DOG
OBEDIENCE
TRAINING

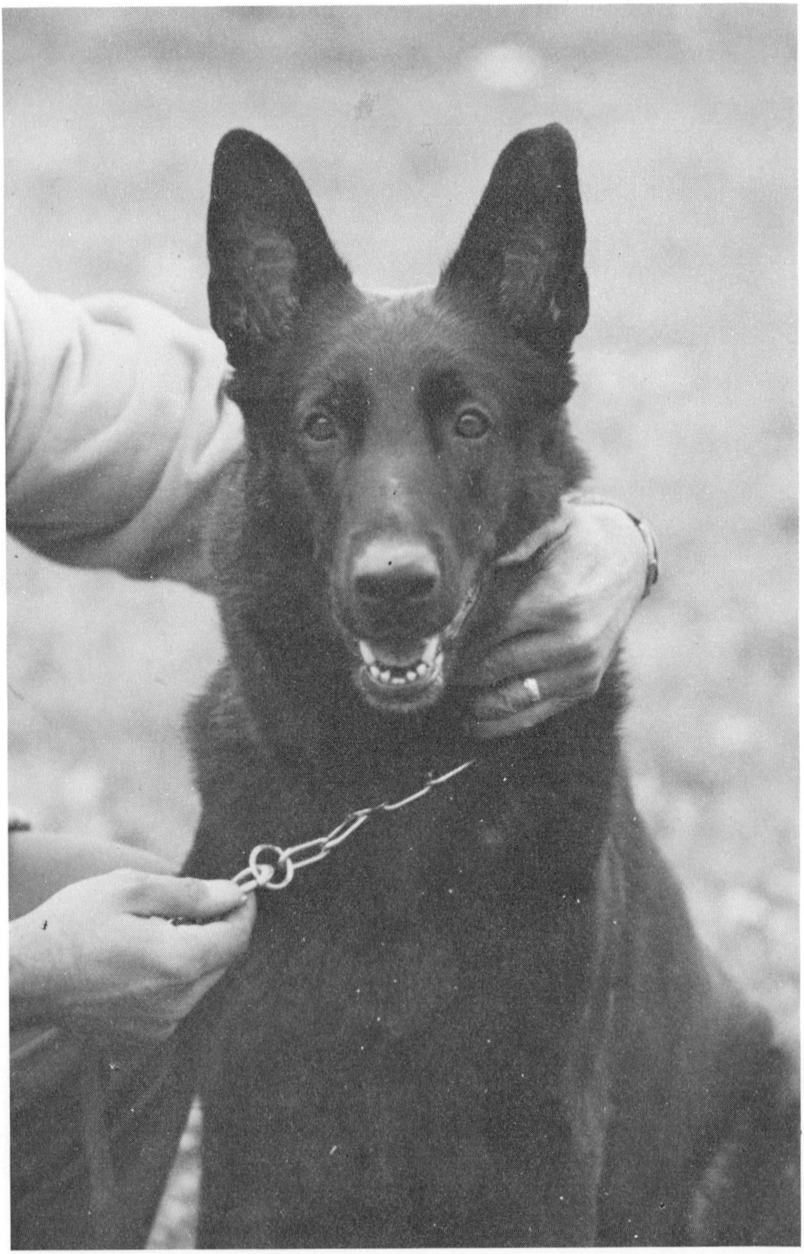

DOG OBEDIENCE TRAINING

Gust Kessopulos

SOUTH BRUNSWICK AND NEW YORK: A. S. BARNES AND COMPANY
LONDON: THOMAS YOSELOFF LTD

© 1974 by A. S. Barnes and Co.

A. S. Barnes and Co., Inc.
Cranbury, New Jersey 08512

Thomas Yoseloff Ltd.
108 New Bond Street
London W1Y OQX, England

Library of Congress Cataloging in Publication Data
Kessopulos, Gust.
   Dog obedience training.

   1. Dogs—Training. I. Title.
SF431.K47   636.7'08'87   73-10524
ISBN 0-498-01415-0

Unless otherwise noted, all photographs in this volume are by Michael D. Fine.

PRINTED IN THE UNITED STATES OF AMERICA

To Topper
"The best of each breed"

(Photo by Don Long)

Contents

	Acknowledgments	9
1.	Timing in Your Training	13
2.	Acquiring a Puppy	17
3.	Lead-Breaking	24
4.	Off-Lead Heeling	42
5.	Sit-Stay	56
6.	The Down-Stay	61
7.	Stand for Examination	65
8.	The Recall	71
9.	The Heel Position	78
10.	Drop on Recall	82
11.	The Sit—Out of Sight	86
12.	Hand Signals	91
13.	The Dumbbell	98
14.	The Jump	115
15.	Broad Jump	136
16.	Scent Discrimination	145
17.	The Send-Out	156
18.	Directed Jumping	160
19.	The Directed Retrieve	166
20.	Yard-Breaking Your Dog	171
21.	The Dog and the Family Automobile	174

22.	Cold Weather Care of the Dog	177
23.	Warm Weather Care of the Dog	180
23.	Attack Training vs Watchdog	183
25.	The Shy Dog	185
	Appendix: Obedience Regulations of the American Kennel Club	189
	Index	213

Acknowledgments

Grateful acknowledgement is made to The American Kennel Club for permitting me to refer to their obedience regulations and to reprint their "Regulations and Standards for Obedience Trials" in this book.

I also extend my appreciation to Paul M. Clapper, editor and publisher of the Louisville (Ohio) *Herald,* for his encouragement and confidence in my ability.

DOG OBEDIENCE TRAINING

1
Timing in Your Training

TO PROPERLY OBEDIENCE-TRAIN A DOG, THE TRAINER MUST SUCcessfully develop through practice, an almost infallible sense of timing. Some individuals seem to already possess this natural ability to respond to a given situation efficiently, others must work at it.

In order to give yourself a fair advantage toward the development of correct timing, read the instructions to each phase of the training procedures carefully. Next, know your own dog! You must not assume that because your dog is a certain size or breed his reactions to training will be relative to those basic traits generally attributed to his physical characteristics. For example, some large, heavy dogs can be very agile, while some of the lighter-weight dogs tend to be sluggish.

Another very important influence on your method of training will be your dog's temperament. Observe your dog's reactions to commands, corrections, and praise; then you can determine the most effective procedures. There are a great many opinions as to why a dog has a certain temperament. Some people believe that a dog's temperament is entirely

The author relaxes with his German Shepherd Zorro.

hereditary; others feel that it depends completely on the environment in which a dog is raised. But, in my opinion, it takes a little bit of both. I therefore conclude that an understanding of the dog's temperament combined with coinciding training processes are the keys to successful training.

Some of you may have a dog that is overly exhuberant.

Your objective with this type of dog is to get him under control while maintaining his zest. No amount of obedience training should ever deter a dog's good qualities. Instead, you should take advantage of them. Start by demanding his constant attention. This is done by giving numerous firm commands while training. Do not burden him with sentences; keep your commands clear, distinct, and repetitious. Make your corrections definite and your praise calm. Your overall attitude should be one of confidence in your own ability accompanied by respect for his joy in living.

A somewhat different type is the shy, fearful dog. This particular personality requires, above all, patience along with a complete understanding of the anxieties this dog is actually experiencing. The most common misfortune that befalls the shy dog is that his tremulous attitude is misconstrued as "meanness." Naturally, he does possess a great deal of apprehension toward strangers. Therefore, when working with this type of dog, your main objective is to instill confidence. In order to achieve your purpose, avoid nurturing his fears. Using good judgment, always expect your commands to be obeyed. As soon as he completes an exercise to your satisfaction, be quick to give him plently of physical praise.

Next, we have the dog who seemingly lacks enthusiasm. This is not to be accepted as a situation that cannot be corrected. Put a little spark in your training by working quickly. You will be surprised to find that the more efficiently you work the dog, the better he responds. Be sure that your handling is in no way hesitant. Check the manner in which you are giving your commands. Make sure that you are not *asking* the dog to perform a function, rather than commanding him to do so. Encourage this type of dog continuously.

The ideal temperament, of course, belongs to the dog that

16/DOG OBEDIENCE TRAINING

Although basically a shy dog, Zorro reflects a confidence that can be obtained through proper training.

likes people, is outgoing to an extent, and still maintains a certain amount of calmness. If you are fortunate enough to associate with this type of dog, then you have an excellent beginning. Don't allow this advantage to escape your grasp. Make every effort to obtain the ever-elusive quality of "perfect timing."

2
Acquiring a Puppy

ONE OF THE FIRST PROJECTS, WHEN SEEKING A PUPPY, SHOULD be a thorough assessment of the responsibilities that go along with him. Choose a dog that will blend best with your particular family. If your space is limited and your intention is to keep the dog in the house, then by all means pick a breed that remains small and sheds very little. On the other hand, many large dogs do make good house pets. If your individual taste leans toward big dogs, don't let the fact that you want to keep him in the house frighten you away from your favorite breed. It is advisable, however, to be sure that your home is roomy enough to allow the full-grown dog freedom of movement.

Before purchasing your future pet, do some research on the different breeds and their individual needs. This way, you can avoid the sad experience of having an unhappy dog and a family who feels he is more of a nuisance than a pleasure. A puppy should be brought into your home with the understanding that he is a permanent member of the family.

Once you have decided on the dog that is right for you,

Samson, a rough-coated St. Bernard. This type of dog makes a fine house pet, providing you are willing to brush him regularly and teach him correct behavior at a young age. (Photo by Don Long)

introduce him to your family; then the next person in his life should be the veterinarian. For the good of all, have him checked to make sure he is healthy. He will require some shots to protect him and your family. You can also get the correct dietary advice from your vet.

Those of you who wish to keep your dog outside, should provide his quarters ahead of time. This way he can become accustomed to them right from the beginning. His outdoor housing should be large enough for him when he is full grown. It must be airtight, partially shaded, and adequate fencing should be considered. It is not advisable to keep a dog tied all the time. This can affect both his health and his temperament.

The indoor dog should have a place that he can call his own. Purchase a crate or kennel for him that can serve as his bed and provide him with a place of confinement until he has learned not to chew. The metal crates are easy to clean and sanitize, and they can serve as a place to feed the puppy so that he will not be interrupted. A crate can also be a safety feature for the young dog, as you can put him there when you have to leave him alone and he cannot get into anything that will harm him. If a puppy is given a crate when he is brought home, he will not look upon this place as a confinement but rather as his own private sanctuary.

Now for the ever-present subject of housebreaking your new puppy. The two most important owner's virtues here are patience and repetition. Housebreaking is, in reality, his first obedience lesson. The same basic principles are applied. There are several methods for this, and many of them are effective. I, personally, have been most successful with the following procedure: Put your puppy outdoors once an hour and immediately following each meal. Only leave him outside for a short time whether he obliges you or not. Then, if he has an accident in the house, simply pick him up calmly and put him outside. You will not accomplish anything by harassing a puppy. You will just frighten him and then the learning process will be hindered rather than helped.

When playing with your new pup, be sure that you do not tease him. There are some individuals, who, quite without thinking, find it amusing to tease a puppy. When something is given to him, allow him to keep it. Do not play with him by giving him a doggie toy and taking it away in a teasing manner. This will lead him to believe that the only way he can obtain something from you is to grab or snatch it. This will not be very amusing when he is fully grown. Another playful error that we sometimes allow is the puppy's nibbling at our fingers. He should be told an emphatic *no* when he attempts to do this. The word *no* spoken with authority should be one of the puppy's first obedience experiences. He will soon learn what this word means and will be quick to respond.

Puppies have a natural need for something on which to chew, due to the simple fact that they must cut their permanent teeth. Not unlike children, they experience pain and will seek relief by chewing on whatever is available to them. Obviously it is advisable to purchase items made especially for dogs to satisfy this need. It is also a good idea to be constantly aware of the young dog's chewing capabilities; keep all shoes and clothing safely put away.

If a puppy does commit an infraction against the household rules, how do you convey your displeasure? As with all obedience training, the puppy should be reprimanded immediately. However, this must be done properly. Use a thinly rolled newspaper and tap the dog on the nose, saying *no* firmly. This should be done only once for each infraction. It is not recommended that you slap a puppy with your hand. A thin newspaper is much more effective because the noise alone will serve your purpose. A young dog is just as vulnerable to injury as a baby. Therefore, you must exercise good judgment at all times. Soon the word *no* alone will be sufficient.

For those of you who acquire a collar for your new dog, be sure that it fits properly. This means that you will probably have to get several different collars before the dog is fully grown. Make sure that it fits tight enough so that the dog cannot slip out of it, but not so tight that it causes discomfort and difficulty in removing. Any type of collar that suits your taste will be sufficient for a puppy.

ACQUIRING A PUPPY/21

The matter of your dog's collar does require some more serious considerations. The dog should not be allowed to wear his collar except when it is actually being used. It is not a decoration for his neck, but a useful piece of equipment. Although tying a dog outside is not recommended, if you must do this for some reason then by all means use a plain leather collar. Do not use the choke collar. The reason

Caesar, a smooth-coated St. Bernard. Keep in mind that a puppy should not take liberties that you would be unwilling to allow in the full-grown dog. (Photo by Don Long)

is self-explanatory: your dog could get caught on something and choke himself. If possible, always supervise your dog when he is tied outside. Be especially careful that you do not forget to remove the dog's collar before placing him in a kennel or crate. Make it a habit to check and be sure the collar is removed before you leave him alone at home. Better still, make a place for it right inside the door and keep it there—except when you are on the other end of a lead.

When raising a puppy, think ahead: Don't allow him to take liberties with your furniture that you will not permit when he is fully grown. A puppy has keen senses and is very quick to establish routines. Take advantage of this instinct. Feed him regularly and exercise him regularly, and it will make your everyday coexistence much simpler. Keep his food and water dishes in the same place all the time. Supply him with plenty of fresh, cold water, especially if he is kept outside in the hot summer.

One of your dog's most important possessions should be his brush. A clean dog is not only more pleasant to have around but he will feel better. Daily brushing is just as important as periodic bathing. A dog's coat has a great many natural oils, and by brushing him faithfully you will accentuate the lustre and remove the dirt. This also stimulates the growth of the coat and prevents shedding. Brushing a puppy will teach him that this is a natural part of his routine and will eliminate struggling with a full-grown dog that doesn't like to be brushed.

Another subject that warrants mention is the handling by children of dogs. If treated properly, this is undoubtedly one of the more rewarding experiences in the life of a child. A child and a puppy must be taught to respect one another. A child should understand that a dog is a living responsibility that cannot be tossed aside when he becomes bored. In turn, the puppy should be taught that a child's toes and fingers are not his to nibble on. This means that the parent is obligated to supervise the proper development of a good relationship between child and dog.

3
Lead-breaking

LEAD-BREAKING YOUR YOUNG DOG IS USUALLY ONE OF THE FIRST undertakingss for most new canine owners. This is one phase of training that does not necessitate specific equipment. Any proper fitting collar will prove satisfactory. Choose whatever type of lead that suits your taste, and whatever length lead between three and six feet is adequate for your size dog. It is my recommendation that most breeds be at least three months of age before beginning this task. If you acquire an older dog, begin as soon at you feel he has adjusted to his new surroundings.

Lead-breaking a dog need not become a dreaded burden, as it can be accomplished with relative ease. The best approach for the novice dog owner is a gradual one. For the first experience, simply put the collar on the dog for about one hour. Then take it off and forget it until the next day.

On the second day, put the collar on the dog for about 30 minutes, at which time you will attach a light lead to the collar and allow the dog to walk around with the lead dragging. You must supervise this portion of the training carefully so that no harm befalls the puppy as he drags the lead about. After approximately 15 minutes, remove both the collar and the lead until the next session.

Repeat this basic procedure the following day, with the exception that you will attach the light lead immediately. After a few minutes have elapsed, pick up the lead. With the dog on your left side, start walking in a normal fashion and encourage the dog to remain with you by giving short tugs on the lead and commanding the dog to *heel*. Depending upon the size and age of your individual dog, exercise your own judgment as to the amount of effort extended. Continue with this procedure for about 15 more minutes and then discontinue until the next day.

Use this method for about 15 minutes a day until your dog

Walk in a normal fashion and encourage the dog to remain with you.

A little defiance is a normal reaction from the dog, and you can counteract this problem with plenty of praise.

Since this is a new experience for the young dog, it is your responsibility to help him develop the proper attitude toward his collar and lead.

becomes accustomed to the lead and to remaining with you. Keep in mind that if your particular dog does not respond to a phase of the training, then you must repeat that segment until he becomes proficient before advancing to the next step. Don't be surprised if your dog suddenly becomes stubborn. He may balk defiantly, throw a tantrum, or even acquire a rather tenacious grip on the lead with his teeth. These are normal reactions for his situation. Your dog is understandably frightened; this is his first encounter with discipline or any form of authority. You can counteract these problems by praising your dog abundantly for every expression toward behavior that he exhibits, no matter how minor.

Remember that your purpose is simply to teach the dog to walk on lead. This is not to be confused with the actual heeling procedure. The only reason that you use the command *heel* during this exercise is to communicate with the dog. For those of you who are ready for regular obedience, it can only prove to be to your advantage. For those who do not wish to teach obedience at this time, it can do no harm. It is most important that your dog develop the proper attitude toward his lead and collar; this is your first responsibility. It will undoubtedly depend a great deal on *your* attitude toward the entire undertaking. You must approach lead-breaking with confidence and patience. Your future training relationship could be affected by the success or failure of this seemingly insignificant enterprise.

Equipment

The first thing you and your canine companion are going to need is the proper equipment. This consists of a choke collar made of either chain or nylon and a six-foot lead, made of mesh or leather. I would recommend leather because of its durability. You can find both of these at any pet supply store near you.

The choke collar should fit comfortably over the dog's head and neck.

Attach the lead to the large link on the outside of the collar.

LEAD-BREAKING/29

The next step is to put your dog's collar on in the proper way. The simplest way to do this is to make a noose with your collar and slip it over the dog's head. It fits correctly if it slips comfortably over the head and neck. Now attach your lead to the large link on the outside. If properly applied, your collar will tighten and loosen when pulled and released by you.

The Beginning Experience

Let us begin the first lesson: Take your lead in both hands. With the dog on your left side, gather the excess lead neatly in your right hand and place your left hand on the lower portion of the lead. Make sure that there is a loop in the lead

To start, make sure the dog is sitting properly at your left side.

Command the dog to heel, *giving the lead a quick snap with your right hand.*

Walk straight forward in a normal fashion, making sure that you allow slack in the lead.

by the dog's neck. This is most important as there should be no tension in the lead.

With the dog sitting on your left side, you are ready for your first steps together. Moving forward with your LEFT foot first command your dog to *heel*, giving your lead a quick snap with your right hand. Take about ten steps in a straight line and stop. When you stop, pull up on the lead with your right hand and press down on the dog's hindquarters with your left hand, commanding the dog to *sit*.

Repeat the previous instructions until you have reached perfection. Read it until you have it memorized, then begin. Remember to be patient, and do not become excited or angry. This is not a game! You are teaching and your dog is learning.

Now start to use the dog's name before the command to *heel*. Say your dog's name to get his attention. Do not allow him to move. If he does not look at you when you say his name, give the lead a gentle snap straight up, saying his name at the same time. When you get his attention, praise him by telling him that he is a good boy, but do not allow him to move. After the dog responds to his name without moving, combine the name with what you have already learned.

Say the dog's name, then move forward with you left foot first, giving the command to *heel* simultaneously. If he does not respond to the word *heel* and your left foot, give a snap of the lead with your right hand, repeating the command *heel*. When you stop, make him sit immediately using the method described previously and be sure to use the word *sit*. Continue this procedure for about two weeks. At the end of that time, the dog should respond to *heel* without being reminded and he should *sit* without being told.

32 / DOG OBEDIENCE TRAINING

To teach the dog to sit, pull up on the lead with your right hand and press down on the dog's hindquarters with your left hand.

Basic Heeling

So far, you have been walking and stopping in a straight line. Let's try something new. You are going to do an about turn: Start walking forward in the normal fashion, then simply turn around and start walking in the opposite direction. At the exact point at which you turn around, give the command to *heel*. Practice this until the dog responds to your turning around without being told to do so.

After you have accomplished this, proceed to right turns. Again, start out in the straight forward position, turn right, and as you turn command the dog to *heel*. In other words, this exercise is handled in the same manner as the about turn.

To execute an about turn, simply turn around and start walking in the opposite direction.

Now you are ready to try a left turn. This is slightly different, because you will be walking *into* your dog rather than *away* from him as you had done on the about turn and the right turn. So, what do you do to handle this situation? Simply turn left, and when you bump into the dog command *heel* and keep on walking. By this time, your dog is learning what the word *heel* means and will soon learn to avoid bumping you on the left turn.

Up to this point, you have been walking at a normal pace. This leaves you with something else to learn about heeling with your dog: the fast and the slow walking pace. When you want the dog to walk slowly, just move very, very, slowly. When he forges ahead of you, command *heel* and give him a quick snap with the lead to bring him to the proper heel position at your left side. The fast pace requires simply the reverse procedure: Break into a run. If he lags behind you, command *heel* and encourage him verbally to catch up with you. For example, pat your leg and say, Come on boy, get up here."

Your training sessions should last only 15 minutes a day—but every day. If time permits, you may have two sessions a day, morning and evening. But remember, only 15 minutes each. A dog's mind tires after this length of time and nothing can be accomplished when he is tired.

These training lessons must be rewarding for both you and your dog. Take time for play periods after the training sessions. Do not play with the dog immediately before a training lesson, and do not use treats during the sessions.

If you follow all of the above instructions carefully, in about six weeks you and your dog will be admired and respected by your family, friends, and neighbors. You are helping him become a better member of society. But, perhaps the most important lesson that can be learned through training your dog will be learned by *you*. You will gain a

When performing the fast pace, you should actually break into a run.

sense of closeness and a relationship between you and your dog that goes way beyond having a nice pet and playmate.

Figure Eight

Using a piece of ordinary chalk, draw an 8 on the ground or whatever floor surface you are working on. It should be eight feet in length. With your dog in the proper heel position, begin by standing about two feet back—facing the intersection of lines in the figure.

Tell your dog to *heel* and start forward. When you reach the chalk line, follow it exactly as you have drawn it—either to the left or right of the figure eight. When you have completed the 8 at least once around, stop and make the dog sit.

Using whatever you have available to simulate the posts, your purpose is to get the dog to perform the fast, normal, and slow paces while the handler maintains the same pace throughout the exercise.

LEAD-BREAKING/37

38/DOG OBEDIENCE TRAINING

Practice your complete figure eight several times, making sure that you periodically stop and require the dog to sit.

Be sure that when you draw your pattern for the figure eight that the open part of the 8 is large enough for a person to stand in.

You will find that the average dog will have a tendency to forge head on the inside turn and to lag on the outside turn. Be ready for this and make the proper corrections with your lead and the command *heel*. When you determine that your dog is performing the figure eight reasonably well, you are ready for the next step. Remember, I stated that you should leave room in your figure eight for a person.

This is the next step—people: Get two members of your family or two of your friends to stand for you. Place them eight feet apart, directly across from each other. You can eliminate your chalk drawing unless you want to measure your distance, and put a couple of X marks for your assistants to stand on. Start out the same way as when you were using your drawing. Stand at an equal distance between the two people—about two feet back—then start forward in either direction. Make your complete figure eight around both individuals and then halt. If you are executing the figure eight properly, you will assume one continuous walking pace throughout the exercise, while the dog must adjust to all three speeds in order to maintain the proper heel position at all times.

After your dog gets practically perfect on the normal figure eight, try stopping beside the individuals who are standing for you. Remember, no sniffing or interest in the person should be allowed. If your dog progresses very well, try to get him accustomed to all individuals.

You are probably wondering about the value of this particular exercise. Well, let's talk about its practical value: You are walking very closely to individuals, requiring your dog to heel properly and pay no attention to them. Never allow your dog to sniff or slow down when walking around the people. If he tries to do either of these things, command *no* followed by *heel*, and, if necessary, a firm snap of the lead. This exercise teaches that while the dog is on command, he cannot be distracted by other people. He must pay no attention to them unless you release him from command.

Perfecting On-Lead Heeling

It is time to take a look at your overall heeling. Because you are about to begin off-lead work, you must make sure that both you and your dog are ready.

Start heeling your dog on lead in the normal manner. Make your left turns, right turns, and about turns. When performing these exercises, there must be constant slack in your lead and your dog must be making every effort to maintain the pace you are setting for him. He should not be forging or lagging.

Be very objective in judging his heeling progress. Do not make compensations for your dog by hurrying up for him when he is forging or slowing down when he is lagging; this is not proper heeling. If you find that you are doing this, there are some corrective measures that *you* must make to prepare for off-lead work.

Moving forward in the normal heeling pattern, make an abrupt about turn. The dog should immediately make the about turn with you. If he does not, give him a quick snap of the lead along with the command *heel*. This same procedure must be used each time the dog is not properly heeling.

You must begin to accept nothing less than perfection in your heeling exercise. This means simply that the dog must give you his complete attention at all times. If he does not, then you cannot possibly hope to keep him obedient off lead.

You and your dog must become a team. If your dog is not heeling properly on lead, there is no way he will do so off lead. For example, if your lead tightens up when you are heeling on lead, just pretend the lead isn't there and imagine where your dog would be if he were not attached to his lead. This should answer any question in your mind about why proper on-lead heeling is a must to prepare for off-lead heeling.

When heeling with your dog, don't forget proper correction combined with proper praise. Talk to your dog when you're walking with him; give him verbal encouragement. This is most important, and it will aid you when you begin off-lead heeling. Although these conversations may seem silly to you, they will keep his attention—which is what you are striving for.

Then test your three speeds: Try your slow, fast, and normal. Make sure he adjusts to your designated speed. If he doesn't, make the proper corrections.

If you have been working your dog faithfully each day, you probably are having only a few minor problems. This is the time to work them out. Remember, it can be done. At this point, it can be done quite easily. But if you haven't been working regularly, don't make the mistake of thinking that you are ready.

I can recall quite a humorous incident in a class I was instructing one time. In it was a gentleman with a German Shepherd dog. I stressed the fact that you should maintain a loose lead. His lead was completely loose; however, I noticed that he had to run constantly to *keep* the lead loose. He was maintaining a loose lead by keeping up with his dog, rather than requiring the dog to heel with him! So, dig in and work out any imperfections in your heeling. This is one exercise that you cannot overdo.

4
Off-lead Heeling

ASSUMING THAT YOUR DOG IS HEELING PROPERLY ON LEAD, YOU can begin heeling your dog off lead. It is advisable to begin off-lead heeling in a confined area like a garage, room, or fenced-in yard.

Start forward from the normal heel position. Then make an about turn. If your dog lags on the about turn, begin to praise your dog; in other words use voice control. Tell him *Good boy* or *get up here*, and use an encouragement such as patting your leg at the same time. If you can see immediately that your dog is not responding, put your lead on the dog and repeat the same procedure using the lead. This time, however, when you make your about turn, snap your lead and say *heel*.

Continue walking forward in the natural heeling pattern, and while doing this simply reach down and unsnap the lead as quickly and inconspicuously as possible. Then make another about turn, using your voice again to encourage and control your dog. If he responds, then continue heeling off lead.

Go on with your normal off-lead heeling in the forward

To start off-lead heeling, simply walk straight forward in the normal fashion.

If the dog begins to get out of control, use your voice command to pull him back to your side.

direction, including some halts. Each time you start forward, don't forget to tell your dog to *heel*. If you find that you are having success, begin to make some left turns and right turns. If necessary, use a few extra *heel* commands. Make your commands firm. However, a firm tone means just that. Do not scream at your dog or snatch at him with your hands in an offensive manner. This is a new experience for him and you must be careful not to frighten or confuse him. Keep calm.

Anytime that you feel your dog is not paying attention, make a turn in the opposite direction. Use your voice to encourage him to remain at your side. Do not hesitate to put the lead on your dog when you feel he is getting out of control. Keep the lead on for only a short time, as stated previously, and then remove it again.

Any time you feel the dog is not paying attention, make a turn in the opposite direction.

While performing the fast pace off-lead, keep your eye on the dog and be ready to give extra verbal commands if necessary.

The next step is to try your fast and slow speeds. Now you know ahead of time what you are going to do, so keep your eyes on your dog and be ready to give a *heel* command if necessary. When he responds, don't forget to praise him verbally. Let him know that he is doing a good job .If he gets out of control during the change of speeds, put that lead back on for a few moments.

Remember, as I have already stated, if your dog fails to respond satisfactorily to off-lead heeling, there is only one cure. Go back to on-lead heeling until your dog no longer tugs and pulls on that lead. You will know that your dog is heeling properly on lead when you feel as if you don't even have a dog at the end of it. Only you can be the judge of this.

For those of you who are having success with off-lead heeling, there are a few things you must remember: Don't become overconfident too soon. Stay in that confined area when doing your off-lead work. He is just beginning and cannot possibly be completely dependable.

The most important thing for you to remember at this point is that even later on when your dog becomes proficient at off-lead heeling, there is no necessity for you to take him on a public street off lead. This should not be permitted. There is no logical reason why your dog should be allowed on a public street off lead; there is always the possibility of that one unfortunate time when something unforseen could happen to distract him and he could bolt away from you.

An Objective View of Heeling

Perhaps it is time that you paused and surveyed your heeling procedures objectively. All of us have a tendency to ignore heeling in favor of the more technical lessons; however, nothing is more relative to an obedient dog than good heeling.

Review some of the more pertinent factors necessary for proper heeling: Start with your left foot first. Remember to give the *heel* command simultaneously with the forward movement of your left foot. If you preface the *heel* command with the dog's name, be sure that you do not move until you actually give the word. Otherwise your dog will develop the habit of moving everytime he hears his name. This is most undesirable.

Now, review some of the specifications that determine whether your dog is heeling efficiently or not. For example, is your dog heeling too widely? A dog that is walking too widely moves one or two feet away from you. This problem can be corrected by giving extra heel commands, and, at the

OFF-LEAD HEELING/47

The dog is heeling too widly when he is one or two feet away from you.

same time, giving a quick snap of the lead to bring him to your side. The important word here is "snap:" It does not mean that you pull the dog, neither does it mean that you jerk the dog severely. Snap the lead, then release the tension immediately. If this is done properly, your dog will soon realize what you want and there will be no further problem.

Watch for the dog that "crowds" the handler: He simply heels too closely and bumps into you all the time. This can be remedied by making a series of left turns. As you make your left turn, walk in a normal fashion directly into the path of your dog. This will quickly convince the dog that you cannot both be in the same spot at the same time. After a few of these left turns, start using a normal heeling procedure and see if he heels correctly. Until it is no longer necessary, supplement your daily heeling pattern with some extra left turns.

The next trait is "forging," when the dog persists in staying ahead of you several feet. More often than not, this is the fault of the handler. When you are heeling on lead, do

A dog is heeling too closely when he forces the handler to move aside to avoid bumping into him; this is crowding.

When the dog races ahead several feet, he is forging.

you find that your lead is usually taut? If your answer is yes, this is why your dog is forging instead of heeling correctly at your side. You are hanging onto him instead of requiring him to heel. Simply employ the basic heeling correction, which is a quick snap of the lead accompanied by the word *heel*. Release the lead instantly and allow him to forge ahead until he reaches the end of the lead and then make another

The dog that consistently heels behind you is lagging.

correction. Just a few effective corrections and you will be amazed how quickly your problem is eliminated.

How about the dog that lags? A dog is lagging when he heels consistently behind you. This can, again, usually be attributed to improper handling and is more common in the heavy breeds. It is natural for them to be a bit lackadaisical. You can remedy this situation by maintaining a normal walking pace. Do not adapt to your dog. You have probably been doing this without realizing it, and by adapting to his slow pace you were accentuating the lagging tendencies. You must demand that the dog accommodate himself to *your* pace in order to obtain proper heeling.

You are undoubtedly aware that during this analysis on heeling, I am constantly referring to the on-lead work. This applies to everyone: Whether you are a beginner or an experienced handler, your dog is never beyond being worked on lead. The better you want him to be, the more you will insist upon working with the dog on lead. When you do work him off lead, you can be reasonably sure that he will heel properly.

Straight Sits

The next object of our attention will be straight sits. Here is another one of those minute points in obedience training that everyone tends to overlook as unimportant. However, for show dogs this is probably the most costly in terms of point deduction.

A straight sit can be defined as one in which the dog is in the heel position, facing the same direction as the handler, with his head area in line with the handler's left hip—as close as possible without interfering with the handler's motion.

Let's discuss the several types of crooked sits and what can be done to correct them. A sit is considered incorrect any time a part of the dog's body touches you. This is called "crowding," the same as in the heeling exercise. One of the best ways to correct this type of sit is to take one step forward, giving the verbal *heel* command, and walk away from the dog, thereby forcing him to straighten his body. If the dog still insists upon leaning against you, revert to the original method of teaching the dog to sit. Holding the lead in your right hand pull upward, and, at the same time, use your left hand to place his hindquarters into position.

A problem, too, is the dog that continuously sits slightly behind you. Often this is the result of a dog that also lags when heeling. To alter this type of sit, you must bring the

The dog that sits slightly behind the handler at an angle is usually guilty of lagging as well.

dog forward to your side, placing him in the proper heel position and at the same time giving the verbal *heel* command several times.

What about the dog that sits too far away from you? We will assume that the dog heels properly but then simply swings away from you the moment you stop. This, more than likely, can be traced to incorrect foot movement on the part of the handler. Make sure that when you halt, you do not stomp your feet. Many handlers do this quite unconsciously, possibly because they try to stop too quickly or perhaps signal the dog that they are going to halt. This will undoubtedly create a negative response from your dog. Just practice stopping in a quiet, smooth manner.

Some dogs will habitually sit at an angle almost directly in front of you. Watch to see if the dog is forging while he is heeling. This is usually the prime cause when the dog sits ahead of you. Another factor that can be involved here is inattention; you must keep his attention at all times. This can be done by talking to the dog during the practice sessions. Once the dog becomes accustomed to paying attention, you can gradually reduce the conversation.

One of the most efficient ways to correct any kind of a poor sit is to anticipate your dog's sits. Analyze your individual situation and prepare to correct a poor sit before it happens. You must also be consistent. That is, correct every poor sit, not just some of them. If you allow your dog to sit crookedly one time and not the next, you will only confuse him. He will understand much more quickly if he is expected to sit straight without exception.

It is also pertinent to use the verbal *heel* command as often as you deem necessary. When a dog is corrected, he must be reminded with a familiar command the reason for being corrected. This will also prove advantageous at a later date, when by simply using the word *heel* the dog will automatically correct himself.

You should also scrutinize your own body movements. Many cases of poor heeling and bad sits can be traced directly to poor handler movements. One of the most common handler errors is walking into your dog. This will cause both wide heeling and crooked sits. Be sure that you are

If the dog heels properly but sits too widely at an angle, it is very often due to improper handling.

walking in an absolutely straight line, and maintain a constant awareness of the problem. Pick out an object across the room or yard that you can use as a guide and practice walking directly toward it.

You are probably thinking that I am very demanding with the handlers. Well, I am. I think that the least we can do for our canine companions is to give our very best efforts to them; in return we receive their patient understanding and complete devotion—in spite of our many human fallacies.

5
Sit-Stay

SINCE BY THIS TIME, YOUR DOG IS SITTING WITHOUT BEING TOLD and heeling fairly well, you are ready to begin what is known as the sit-stay exercise.

As with any exercise, begin with the dog sitting in the proper heel position at your left side. With your left hand placed directly in front of the dog's face, give the command *stay*. Be very precise about giving the hand signal. Be sure your hand is open, pointed directly toward the ground with your fingers closed together. Always give this hand signal in exactly the same manner.

Give the command *stay*, using a firm tone of voice simultaneously with the hand signal in the manner described. Pivot directly in front of the dog, and I do mean DIRECTLY in front of the dog. Now, for the obvious, what do you do when the dog decides he will not remain in the stay position? Simply, but firmly, pull straight up on the lead and quickly say *no, sit-stay*. You can do this, as you are standing directly in front of the dog. Once you have accomplished this, then do the reverse. Give the same hand signal, command *stay*, and pivot back to your dog. You and your dog should be

Pivot directly in front of the dog.

If your dog does not remain in the stay position, simply pull straight up on the lead and command no, sit-stay.

facing in the same direction with the dog at heel.

Practice this until your dog is completely dependable on responding to the word *stay*. Now you are ready to leave your dog for about three feet. If you are using the recommended six-foot lead, we refer to this as "half a lead length." Give the hand signal and the command to *stay* and walk away from the dog with your right foot first. At this point, you are approximately three feet away from your dog. If the dog does not remain in the stay position, remember the previously indicated correction—with one additional move necessary on your part. Simply take a step into your dog as you perform the required corrections.

The next step is to get back to the dog from this distance. Repeat the word *stay* giving the proper hand signal and walk briskly around the dog into the correct heel position. Be careful to hold your lead away from the dog's body and face. You should be holding the majority of the lead in your right hand, so just lift the balance of the lead with your left hand over the dog's body. Remember not to allow the lead to tighten around the dog's neck at any time during this procedure.

When you and your dog have perfected the distance of half a lead length you are ready for the full six feet of the lead. If a reminder is needed, respond in the same manner as you would from the three-foot distance. Step into the dog and make the correction. Return to the dog in the same manner to the heel position.

This exercise can often be of great value during your daily routine. For example, the individual who is feeding your pet can tell him to *sit-stay* while placing his food and water in front of him. This can be especially helpful if you happen to be cleaned up to go somewhere. It is also very pleasing to guests when they see your well-behaved dog remaining in a particular place while they are visiting.

Leave your dog a full lead length away and stand facing the dog, making sure that the leads are off the ground but not taut.

Are you remembering to praise your dog when he performs an exercise correctly? Praise is just as important as correction. It is especially important to praise your dog for doing something properly after he has been corrected. This is one of the ways that you communicate to him the difference between right and wrong.

This is a most important factor for any good dog trainer to remember: A well-adjusted and happy dog knows what is right and what is wrong. A spoiled dog does not.

I cannot remind you enough that patience is a virtue. Read the directions carefully so that you fully understand what you want to accomplish; *then* begin training your dog. Teach properly, make your corrections properly, and he will learn. Improper training can cause your dog to become confused and unhappy. Don't blame your dog for not learning if you are not teaching correctly. This is certainly a great disservice to a dog whose only aim is to please you.

6
The Down-Stay

YOU WILL BEGIN, AS ALWAYS, WITH THE DOG SITTING IN THE proper heel position. Then, take your lead and place it neatly on the ground beside the dog. This is done to prevent the lead from becoming tangled and getting in your way while you are trying to teach the initial phases of the exercise.

The next step is to get on your knees beside your sitting dog. Place your left arm around the dog's body directly behind the dog's left front leg with your other hand directly behind the dog's right front leg. Gently lift the dog's front legs simultaneously out from under him and at the same time repeat the word *down* several times. As soon as the dog is completely down, stay with him, giving him the command *stay*.

This particular step in the training process will give the dog a rather unsteady feeling; therefore, your motions must be deliberate and executed with absolute perfection. Once the dog is in the down position, take your left hand and stroke his back, all the while repeating the command *stay*. This will give him the reassurance that he needs at this point.

Gently lift the dog's front legs (simultaneously) out from under him.

As the dog remains in the down position, take your left hand and stroke his back, repeating the command stay.

Keeping your left hand gently placed on the dog's body, gradually lift yourself to a standing position, repeating the *stay* command. As you reach the standing position, remove your hand from the dog's body and stand completely erect. If the dog remains in the down position, simply kneel beside him again and stroke his back, praising him calmly for being a good dog. Repeat the *down-stay* commands and stand up again.

If the dog remains in position, you may then take one step forward and give the command to *heel*. Repeat this entire routine until you have reached perfection.

Once the dog becomes dependable, try to get him to go *down* on command only. Start with your dog in the correct heel position, and, with your right hand in front of the dog's face, give a downward sweeping motion using the command *down*. If the dog fails to respond he is not ready for this phase of training, and you must start from the beginning until he grasps the purpose of the entire procedure.

After you have accomplished getting the dog to go down on command, then you are ready for the pivot in front of your dog while he is in the down position. You will, of course, hold the lead in the normal manner at this time. Commencing with the dog in the heel position, put your dog down, then pivot directly in front of the dog. To get back to the proper heel position, simply pivot back to your dog.

When the dog becomes dependable on the down with you directly in front of him, you are ready to leave him half a lead length or three feet. Put your dog down, command him to *stay*, then leave your dog. Return to your dog in the usual manner. Hold the lead with your right hand and with your left hand gently lift the lead over the dog's body. Remember, don't allow the lead to tighten or touch the dog.

As soon as you have accomplished this you are ready for the full lead length or six feet. Perform this portion of the

64 / DOG OBEDIENCE TRAINING

If the dog breaks position when you are a full lead length away you can correct this by simply stepping into him and smartly snapping the lead downward.

exercise in exactly the same way as the three-foot distance. This will be one of the more difficult exercises to execute, so don't allow yourself to become impatient. It takes time.

If at any time the dog breaks position, the best way to make the correction is to return to the dog and start over again. You cannot make an effective correction from a distance. Trying to do this will simply confuse the dog and cause the exercise to seem more difficult than it really is. Don't ever hesitate to take enough time to teach an exercise correctly, as opposed to settling for half-way measures.

7
Stand for Examination

THE STAND FOR EXAMINATION CAN BE A REASONABLY SIMPLE exercise to teach—if you proceed patiently with the fundamental steps: First, begin heeling the dog in the normal manner, then, just before you come to a halt, prevent the dog from performing the automatic sit.

This is done by placing your left hand in front of his left hind leg and giving the command *stand*, followed quickly with the *stay* command. You will be holding the lead in your right hand. If your dog has been properly trained thus far, his natural impulse will be to sit. You must prevent him from doing this. To help you accomplish this, put the commands *no* and *stay* to work for you. In other words, when he starts to sit touch his left hind leg, repeating *stand-stay*. If he insists upon sitting, then command *no, stand-stay* and simultaneously touch his hind leg.

If your dog absolutely refuses to remain standing, DO NOT try to physically hold him up; you may hurt or anger him. Simply take a step forward, to get the dog on his feet, and repeat the entire procedure. Once he begins to respond to the *stand*, tell him in a soothing voice that he is a *good boy*

If you are using the lead, place your left hand on the dog's left hind leg while pulling upward on the lead.

Without using the lead, place your left hand on the dog's left hind leg while placing your right hand in the chest area.

STAND FOR EXAMINATION / 67

and stroke his back gently as he is standing. Most dogs enjoy getting their backs scratched and will remain standing. This also accustoms the dog to being touched while he is standing.

When the dog becomes reasonably dependable on the *stand* you are ready for the pivot in front. Command the dog to *stay*, and pivot directly in front of your standing dog. Repeat the *stay* command, and pivot back into the proper heel position. Be sure the dog does not sit when you pivot back. You may find that he will have a tendency to do this. If he does sit or move in any way, give the *no* command and start all over again.

After he will remain standing for the pivot in front, you may then leave him half a lead length. Follow the same

As soon as the dog is reasonably dependable on the stand, you may pivot directly in front of him.

When the dog becomes proficient, you may leave him a full lead length away.

Upon returning from the six-foot distance, hold the lead away from his body and allow plenty of slack.

procedure. Once this is successsful, go the full lead length or six feet. Upon returning from the three or six feet distance, be careful, as always, with your lead. Hold it away from his body, but do not apply any tension.

Once you are absolutely positive the dog knows what is expected of him and will remain standing without reservation, then you may allow another member of the family to inspect the dog by approaching him from the front and touching his head, back, and hindquarters gently. This is the actual stand for examination. I do recommend, however, that at this point and time in your training you allow only members of the household to go over the dog. The reason is simply that some of you may have shy or overexhuberant

Lancer allows the author to examine him, while Mrs. Kessopulos stands facing the dog from a distance of about six feet.

dogs and these particular dogs will require more extensive training and guidance for the handlers before it would be advisable for strangers to attempt to examine them (see chapter on shy dogs).

The *stand* can be one of the most useful exercises in your daily routine around the house. For example, you can stand the dog so that he may be brushed. It will make the task of brushing and grooming the dog no longer a dreaded chore, but rather a pleasure for both you and the dog

8
The Recall

BECAUSE OF THE IMPORTANCE OF TEACHING ONE'S DOG TO come when called, it is imperative that you progress step by step until you reach the point of absolute dependability. A particular exercise must get a positive response immediately. There is no room for hesitation when you command your dog to *come*. He should be so well trained that there would be no question in his mind but to obey this command.

To attain this goal, you will begin with the dog on lead, sitting in the proper heel position. Give the *stay* commands, both verbal and hand signal, and walk away from your dog the full lead length, starting with your right foot first. Setting a precedence of using the proper foot work is very important at this stage in your training, as your dog is beginning to become accustomed to using your left foot as a guide in knowing when to heel with you. Keeping a slight slack in the lead, turn and face your dog. Hesitate, then, using the dog's name, follow immediately with the word *come*, simultaneously give a snap of the lead toward you. This will force the dog to rise and start moving toward you. You may repeat the word *come* as many times as you deem

With a slight slack in the lead, stand facing your dog.

Give the command come *while simultaneously giving a snap of the lead.*

Be sure to gather the lead neatly as the dog approaches; this avoids any possibility of the dog tripping over the lead.

it necessary. Gather the lead in your hands as he approaches the correct front position.

When the dog is directly in front of you, command *sit*. If the dog fails to sit, quickly pull up on the lead and command *sit* again. If the dog sits promptly but favors either the left or right side, rather than the direct front position, then back up and guide him to the front position. This correction should be accompanied by the word *front* repeated several times. Soon, he will learn what the word *front* means, and the command itself will be all that is necessary to obtain the desired position. At this point, praise your dog verbally. Then command him to *stay* and return to him in the normal manner.

When the dog is directly in front of you, command sit.

After you have practiced the indicated method a few times, you will probably find that you can eliminate jerking the lead to get the dog started. He will begin to respond to the word *come* without being forced. When you see this happening, be sure to respond to him by giving him a chance to come on his own. The same holds true when he reaches you; give him a chance to sit without being told. As for the back peddling, use your own judgment. When the dog is coming nice and straight, eliminate that phase.

As you can see, this particular exercise requires more space to practice in than the previous ones. Be sure to take this into consideration and give yourself plenty of room for the freedom of movement necessary to properly maneuver the dog. Your main objective for the first few sessions is to familiarize the dog with the word *come*.

One of the most important facts to remember concerning the recall, is that under no circumstances will you ever punish your dog in any way when he comes to you after being called. The reason is simple: If he finds it to be an unpleasant experience to come to you, then you cannot expect him to obey the recall. If, on the other hand, he finds out that it pleases you, he will be most happy to obey. Don't hesitate to follow a correction with immediate praise. It is more important at the time of a correction than during a normal performance. The difference between right and wrong must be conveyed to the dog. This can be done effectively only if you share your disappointment when an exercise is done poorly and share your joy when it is done properly.

The Recall—Off Lead

The off-lead recall should not be attempted until you feel you have reached perfection on lead. By perfection, I am referring to the dog's prompt response to your commands with no hesitation, a reasonably straight sit in front, and under no circumstances a lack of response to your very first command to *come*. If you can, from an objective point of view, give yourself an affirmative answer to these requirements, then you are ready to begin.

The off-lead recall should be practiced at short distances in the beginning so that you maintain complete control of your dog at all times. It is advisable to use a confined area, such as your garage, for the first few days of this off-lead experience. Proceed in exactly the same manner as you would if your dog was still on lead. Command him to *stay* and leave him for about six feet, then turn and face your dog. Use his name, followed by the word *come*. Require him to sit straight in *front*, and, giving the command *stay*, return to him in the usual manner. Repeat this entire procedure, gradually increasing your distances until, after a reasonable amount of time, you have accomplished a distance of about 30 feet.

Do not hesitate to go back on lead if you are experiencing difficulty of any kind. Keep in mind that it is much easier to execute a proper correction if the dog is put on lead. Only after you have completely mastered the short off-lead recall should you attempt distances of 15 to 30 feet. In addition to learning the basic exercise, the most important feature for the trainer of the off-lead work is voice control. Your commands must be firm and demanding, but tempered with good common sense. Just as a dog will not respond to half-hearted commands, he cannot respond to loud screaming commands with anything but utter confusion.

Next, consider your training problems; we all have them. One of the most common is that of the dog who becomes distracted and disobeys your command to *come*. This situation can be handled in only one way: Put the dog on lead and begin again. Practice under all kinds of conditions until he realizes that he must obey regardless of how interesting some distractions may become. Another problem pertains to the dog that will bolt away from you. If you are sure that you have done nothing to cause this adverse reaction, just walk patiently after him, and when you reach his location, put him on lead and heel him to the exact spot from which he broke. Then repeat the recall exercise on lead a few times. This will soon prove to him that there is no advantage in running away because he must still do what you wanted him to anyway.

If your dog should at any time run to other individuals after you have called him, ask them to ignore him. If they should show any interest in his presence, they will unconsciously be praising him for disobeying you. This, in turn, would encourage this type of behavior every time strangers were present. Some of you may have found that your dog will move out with you when you want him to remain stationary. To avoid this, just pivot directly in front of him, commanding him to *stay*, and return to the heel position. Do this several times until he gets the idea.

Some of you may experience a problem with anticipation, when the dog gets up and starts to come the instant you turn to face him. This has a relatively easy solution: Just put him on lead, and with your left hand take a step toward the dog; use your right hand to pull up on the lead, and give the *sit* command at the same time. Then return to him without calling him. Repeat this as often as necessary.

Be sure to keep this exercise in its proper perspective. Do not get overly anxious to give it the supreme test of an open area outdoors. However, when you feel you are ready for outdoor work, start on lead again. Then use the previously described methods and work your way to the point of an off-lead recall in the backyard.

9
The Heel Position

THUS FAR, WHEN REFERRING TO THE HEEL POSITION, YOU HAVE started out with your dog sitting at your left side. You are going to teach your dog to assume this position when instructed to do so.

Before beginning this particular exercise, check your choke collar. Make absolutely sure that you have it on properly and that the collar and lead are in perfect position.

Then take the excess lead in your right hand, as always, but put your left hand near the end of the lead. Leave some slack in the lead as you normally would.

With your dog sitting in the normal heel position, pivot in front of your dog. Next, take a look at your own feet. You should be standing with both feet together, directly in front of your dog. Keeping your right foot firmly in place, move your left foot backward one step, simultaneously moving your dog from in front of you with a counterclockwise motion into the proper heel position. At the same time, bring your left foot back into position. This exercise must be performed very rapidly. However, the movement should be smooth and swift, not sluggish. You should repeat the word *heel* several times as you are putting the dog in position. Once the dog begins to show genuine response to this entire procedure, eliminate moving your feet. Simply use your lead and the word *heel*.

To prepare for this particular lesson it might be a good idea not only to read the instructions very carefully but to practice your own movements without the dog a few times. As in all obedience-training, your timing and performance are just as important as the dog's.

When you feel that both you and the dog have perfected this exercise, then you are ready to take the lead off. Once again, I remind you, begin in a confined area. Simply pivot in front of your dog and command him to *heel*. If you have properly taught him this lesson, he will automatically respond to the word *heel* and go to the proper heel position at your left side.

You may now combine this exercise with many of the previous ones, such as the recall. When your dog comes to you and sits in front of you, from now on, tell him to *heel*. He will then end up sitting neatly beside you. This is just one instance when it can be used. You will find it very useful (as well as rather smart looking) in conjunction with just about any exercise.

Teaching the dog to assume the heel position.

THE HEEL POSITION/81

10
Drop on Recall

SINCE YOUR DOG HAS ALREADY LEARNED THE RECALL AND should by now be responding to the down command, let's combine the two exercises so that we can "down" the dog after calling him. In obedience terms it is called the "drop on recall."

To begin, have the dog on lead, sitting in the correct heel position. Command the dog to *stay* and leave him one full lead length away. Facing your dog and holding the lead in both hands, command the dog to *come*. As the dog starts to move toward you, back peddle quickly—preventing the dog from catching up to you. Then abruptly command the dog *down* and simultaneously snap the lead downward.

As soon as the dog's body touches the ground, tell him to *stay*. Return to the dog, bend down and calmly praise him, but require him to remain in the down position. Tell the dog to *stay* and leave him again, the full lead length. After you turn to face your dog, hesitate for a moment, then command the dog to *come*. Make sure that he sits in front of you immediately when he comes in. Finish the exercise with lots of praise.

Practice this as many times as necessary. When the dog is reacting promptly to the verbal *down* command, then you should eliminate snapping the lead. When you feel that you and the dog are coordinating with reasonable efficiency on lead, then you may progress to off-lead training.

Commencing with the off-lead portion of the exercise, you will use the hand signal along with the verbal command. Keep in mind that to be effective you should not leave your dog for long distances just yet. A length of eight or ten feet is far enough. When you are in the appropriate position, command your dog to *come*. As he approaches, throw your right arm and hand straight upward and continue with a downward sweeping motion accompanied by the verbal

Use both the hand signal and the verbal command until the dog becomes proficient.

down command. Make sure that your hand signal is always the same and that it is one continuously smooth motion. You must proceed just as you did on lead. Return to the dog, praise him, leave him again, and finish the recall.

Extend your distances gradually. You should eventually reach approximately 40 feet. Once the dog obeys the *down* command faithfully, the most common problem that exists is slowness. You can combat this with firm confident commands and lots of happy, sincere praise given at proper intervals. It is not the purpose of this exercise to just get the dog to obey the down command; he must react without hesitation to each and every command.

Those who intend to show their dog in competition must eliminate either the hand signal or the voice command. Use of both, simultaneously, is not permitted in the show ring. Be sure to use both signal and voice while training, and when the dog becomes proficient alternate them and decide which gives you the best performance from your dog. For practical purposes around the home, use whatever is best for the particular circumstance involved.

A problem that is sometimes encountered with this exercise is "walking" after the down command is given. The dog usually drops as per your command—but where and when he pleases. This is not to be permitted. If the exercise is to be of any practical value, the dog must respond immediately. If you find that this is happening to you, check the way in which you are giving your commands. Usually, you will find that you are not being very emphatic vocally. Not loud, emphatic. Excessive loudness will only cause unfavorable reactions from your dog. Use a sharp *down* command in a normal tone of voice. Do not drag the word out. You will be surprised to find that something as seemingly unimportant as succinct commands can make the difference between success and failure.

Regardless of the dog's size, he must respond immediately to the down *command.*

There is another fact about this exercise that could be of subsequent importance. Once the dog has sufficiently learned the entire procedure, do not make a habit of dropping the dog every time you call him. If you do, he will soon begin to anticipate the down command. So be sure to alternate the drop with the straight recall.

11
The Sit-Out of Sight

IN ONE OF THE PREVIOUS LESSONS, THE DOG WAS TAUGHT TO sit–stay on command. We discussed the practical purposes of this exercise such as convenience in feeding the dog. Now it is time to go a little further with this particular exercise. Since you have begun off-lead work, you have opened the door to something new on the sit–stay exercise. It is termed "the sit–stay—out of sight."

Begin this exercise as in all of the off-lead exercises, in a confined area. Put your dog in the sit–stay position. Be sure to use the word *stay* along with the hand signal. Then, leaving on your right foot, walk about 30 feet away from the dog. Upon reaching this distance, turn and face your dog. Be very cautious not to make any gestures that could be construed as any kind of signal to your dog. This could cause the dog to break the sit–stay position.

For the next phase of this exercise, you will need the help of a friend or member of the family. Have someone to walk around the area where the dog is sitting. By this, I do not mean that he should in any way disturb the dog by touching him or directing any motions or conversation to him.

THE SIT-OUT OF SIGHT/87

The sit *with the handlers facing the dogs about 30 feet away.*

The down *with the handlers facing the dogs about 30 feet away.*

Simply ask the person to ignore the dog and walk around as if he were coming across the yard to visit with you.

Watch your dog: he should not be allowed to move any part of his body except his head. He should not be permitted to even move one paw. If he does, very calmly (but swiftly) return to him and physically place him in his original position.

In other words, if your dog moves even slightly in any direction from his original position, you must replace him in the direction from whence he came. He must understand that he has done something wrong, and by not allowing him to see what it was he turned to see, he will soon catch on.

Start by performing this particular exercise for one minute,

The sit *with the handlers completely out of the dog's sight.*

The down *with the handlers completely out of the dog's sight.*

then extend it to three minutes, and finally to no more than five minutes.

After you have perfected this portion of the exercise, you are ready to begin going out of the dog's sight. Place the dog on the *sit–stay* as stated previously. Then walk directly away from the dog in a straight line, a reaasonable distance away. At this point you should have a predetermined point at which you will be out of his sight. You must choose a place that allows you to see the dog without him being able to see you.

The same rules apply; if your dog moves slightly at any time, you may give him a firm command of *no* from your hidden position. However, if he breaks position, you must return to him from your place of hiding and make a correc-

90 / DOG OBEDIENCE TRAINING

tion by replacing him in his original position. Proceed using the approximate same time elements as used before—never more than five minutes.

12
Hand Signals

BECAUSE WHAT YOU ARE GOING TO ATTEMPT IS SOMEWHAT challenging, start slowly and work gradually into the more difficult stages. The first portion of the work is going to be all on lead. You are going to teach the dog the hand signals without using voice commands.

Begin with your dog in the proper heel position. Give both the hand signal and the verbal command to *stay*, and walk a lead length away. Turn, facing your dog, using the previously learned down hand signal and the verbal command—down your dog. If, for any reason, your dog does not respond to the commands, step into your dog using both commands and place your right hand on the lead forcing the dog into the down position. Be sure to praise your dog regardless of whether he obeyed immediately or after your correction. Try not to excite your dog with overexhuberant praise, keep him calm. Insist that your dog remain in the down position for at least 30 seconds. Return to your dog. Repeat this portion of the exercise several times.

When your dog reaches the point when he will go down on the hand signal only, without any verbal command, you are then ready for the second portion of the exercise. Using hand signals only, give your dog the *stay* command, walk away a full lead length, turn facing the dog, and give your dog the hand signal to down. When you have completed this, take your left hand and, with an upward sweeping motion, come in contact with the lead and at that instant give the verbal command to *sit*. If the dog fails to respond, and most likely he will, then you must force him to sit. Again, practice this until you have reached perfection. That is, your dog must sit by means of the hand signal only.

For the third and final phase of the training, let's begin again by leaving the dog, downing him, and sitting him all by means of hand signals only. You are now ready for the recall. The hand signal for the recall is very easy. Simply start with your right arm extended straight out, parallel with your shoulder, and with a smooth sweeping motion bring your arm to rest on your chest. Simultaneously, you must use your verbal command (the dog's name and the command to *come*). Obviously you must be holding your lead in your left hand. You should expect the same perfection on this recall as the ones that you have taught your dog thus far. You must practice this until he comes to you on the hand signal only without having to hear his name or the word come.

Once you have perfected each one of the three phases of this lesson, put them together. In other words, you should be able to leave your dog, down your dog, sit your dog, and call your dog without having to utter a single verbal command. Please remember that for now this must all be done on lead.

Don't be surprised or disscouraged if your dog fails to respond immediately to this new work. It may seem simple enough, but you must remember that you are learning something new just as your dog is. So don't rush into these exercises without reading the instructions carefully. Make sure your signals are clear and consistent.

You must also remember in the beginning when you are still using the verbal commands as well as the hand signals that your timing must be absolutely perfect in combining the two. If it is not, then you could be guilty of confusing the dog.

Hand Signals—Off Lead

Having had success with working on lead hand signals, you are now ready for the more advanced stages.

Needless to say, begin with the dog in the proper heel position. Remove your lead and put it aside. Still using both the verbal command and the hand signals from the previous lesson, leave your dog, but only for about six feet. From this short distance, give your dog all the hand signals in the proper sequence along with the verbal commands. Repeat these exercises several times until you are quite sure that your dog will down, sit, and come to you without hesitation.

When you feel that your dog is responding with confidence to these commands, you are ready for the next step, which is the elimination of the verbal commands. Still leaving your dog only the short distance of six feet, use hand signals only for all the exercises. If your dog fails to respond to any one of the commands, then put him back on lead. There is no other solution for this problem. Practice giving him the commands both verbal and hand signals once, then still on lead, use hand signals only the second time. This should be enough to remind him. Then take him off lead and try again. Once you have achieved perfection at this distance, gradually increase the distance until you have reached a maximum distance of about 30 feet.

There is one additional hand signal for you to begin using at this time. After calling your dog and he is sitting directly in front of you, it is time to teach him the hand signal to go to the heel position.

Some time ago, you taught the dog to go to heel using the verbal command. Now, working with the dog off lead, you are going to accomplish the same thing by using the left hand in the same counterclockwise motion (used in the original heel position exercise) and commanding the dog to *heel*. After several combinations of both the verbal and hand signal commands, eliminate the verbal command to *heel* and use the counterclockwise hand signal by itself.

This is one of those exercises that depends so much on timing and consistency on your part. By this, I mean that your hand signals must be exactly the same each time they are given. You must make sure that you have the dog's attention before giving a hand signal. It is also most important that you do not allow problems to develop because you will not admit that your dog needs to be put back on lead and reminded of what you want. Your final goal will be accomplished much sooner if you will progress slowly but surely.

You will find that this particular exercise is not only impressive, but contains some very practical purposes, as does all obedience work. For example, if for any reason your dog cannot hear a verbal command, he can be given a hand signal that will prove just as effective.

Another important factor for you to remember at this time is that hand signals are only one part of your overall obedience work. They should not replace your verbal commands. No one lesson really replaces another.

THE STAND

THE DOWN

THE SIT

THE RECALL

THE HEEL OR FINISH

13
The Dumbbell

Part One

ONE OF THE MOST INTERESTING FACETS OF OBEDIENCE TRAINING is teaching your dog to accept, hold, and eventually retrieve an object. The first item on the agenda is obtain the proper equipment, which in obedience terms is called a "dumbbell." This is a wooden dowel joined at each end by a wooden block that can be purchased at any pet store near you. Be careful that the dumbbell is the proper size for your individual dog. Just inform the clerk in the store as to the breed of dog that you have and he will be able to help you pick the proper dumbbell. For those of you to whom a dumbbell is not readily accessible, there is an alternate solution: Simply roll a newspaper into a cylindrical shape and bind with some type of tape. Again, please be sure that you use the proper amount of newspaper for the size of your dog's mouth. It would be better to have a dumbbell too small as opposed to having one that is too large.

There are probably some of you who feel that your dog already knows how to take a dumbbell and retrieve it. You

Your first goal is to obtain the proper-fitting dumbbell for your particular dog.

can throw a ball and your dog runs after it quite vigorously and brings it to you. But, stop and think, what would your dog do if you demanded that he perform this particular function on command only? In all honesty, you must admit that your dog is simply playing.

There are many suggested methods pertaining to this particular obedience exercise. Some people base theirs strictly on the "play" method, others do not believe that this is effective and I happen to be one of them. It is my opinion that allowing your dog to play with the dumbbell will prevent him from being completely dependable.

This particular exercise is often abandoned by those who consider it to be impossible. This is simply not true. If your dog is taught properly, he *will* learn to take the dumbbell and eventually retrieve it. Some will respond more readily than others as in all exercises. You have seen the word "patience" in this book more than once, and I cannot emphasize its necessity more than in this particular exercise. The dog that does not respond is undoubtedly the unfortunate victim of the handler's inadequacies.

To begin the basic exercise, put the lead on the dog and have him sitting in the proper heel position. Lay the lead on the ground; be sure there is enough slack in the lead, but not enough to allow the dog to get away from you. Put your left foot on the lead to hold it in place. Take your left hand, using your index finger and your thumb, and place it over the top of the dog's muzzle. Gently pry his mouth open, inserting the dumbbell behind the canine teeth. (The ca-

The dumbbell should be placed behind the canine teeth.

nine teeth are commonly referred to as fangs.) Simultaneously, command the dog using the word *take*. Repeat this command several times. Immediately after the dumbbell is inserted into the dog's mouth, using your right hand, hold his head upwards stroking his lower jaw. At this point, repeat the word *hold* several times. Allow the dog to hold the dumbbell approximately five seconds, then with both hands placed on the ends of the dumbbell, using the word *out*, remove the dumbbell from the dog's mouth. If your dog refuses to release the dumbbell, gently reopen his mouth in the same manner used to insert the dumbbell, still using the command *out*.

As mentioned previously, after the dumbbell is inserted into the dog's mouth, his head is to be held upward. Obvi-

Gently open the dog's mouth and insert the dumbbell.

Be sure to hold the dog's head in an upward position after inserting the dumbbell.

ously, if you allow him to lower his head, the dumbbell will fall out and your entire purpose will be defeated.

When working with the dumbbell in the dog's mouth, gentleness is an absolute must. You cannot expect a dog to perform an exercise if he is being abused. By this, I simply mean that it would be easy to hurt your dog unknowingly, if you are not very careful. Don't bump his teeth or his tongue in any way.

There is another aspect of this particular exercise that is somewhat different from the prior ones: When working with the dumbbell for now, do just that. For about ten minutes only, just work with teaching your dog to take the dumbbell. Forget all other training. If time permits later in the day, you may work any other exercises as usual, but no dumbbell work at that time.

Part Two

Assuming that you have been successful thus far in getting your dog to accept and hold the dumbbell, you are ready for the next step of the exercise: getting your dog to reach out for the dumbbell.

This portion of the exercise will be different in that the dog must, of his own volition, take the dumbbell from you. You have been placing the dumbbell into the dog's mouth up to this point. Now he must reach for it. This part of the exercise will require even more patience and concentration on your part.

Begin with the dog in the proper heel position. Be sure to have him on lead. Take the dumbbell in your right hand and hold it about six inches from the dog. Command him to *take*, repeating the command several times. If the dog fails to respond, then, using your left hand, gently pull him forward toward the dumbbell, repeating the command *take*. Do not move the dumbbell to the dog, make him reach out to get it. At the exact moment the dog shows reaction to the dumbbell, begin to praise him for doing the right thing. (By reaction, I mean starting to open his mouth in an effort to take the dumbbell.)

In this particular exercise, I must emphasize proper handling on *your* part. Caution has to be exercised so as not to bump the dog's mouth at any time with the dumbbell in a menacing manner. He must always associate pleasure with the dumbbell.

At this point in training, when the dog takes the dumbbell do just as you did before; stroke him under the lower jaw with your right hand. Repeat the command *hold* while

If the dog fails to take the dumbbell of his own volition, use your left hand and gently pull him forward toward the dumbbell.

performing this function. After he holds the dumbbell for a few seconds, remove the dumbbell from his mouth with both hands, using the command *out*.

Repeat this portion of the exercise as many times as necessary until he will reach for the dumbbell without being forced by you in any way. When he is just responding to verbal commands, you are ready to extend the distance until you reach a complete arm length.

Once you see that he will reach this complete distance for the dumbbell, then your are ready for the next step: Walk with the dumbbell in your right hand, throw the dog's lead over your shoulder and have him heeling with you, then command him to *take* while walking. The minute the dog reaches for the dumbbell, begin to praise abundantly, keeping him under control at all times. Be sure, when working with this portion of the exercise, that you hold the dumbbell directly in front of the dog's face or lower.

When the dog successfully takes the dumbbell while walking, require him to walk at heel, carrying the dumbbell for a few steps. Just as you are about to halt, remind him to *hold*, then as you halt he should sit as usual in the proper heel position with the dumbbell still in his mouth. Then tell him to *stay* and pivot directly in front of the dog. Reach down and with both hands remove the dumbbell using the command out.

As stated before, the dog should associate pleasure when working with the dumbbell, however, do not allow him to think of the dumbbell as a toy. He must respect it as part of his training equipment. Therefore, when you are finished with this portion of your training each day, put the dumbbell away in a place where the dog cannot possibly find it accidentally and play with it.

A great many dogs do not seem overly enthusiastic toward this particular exercise in the beginning. Therefore, if you are experiencing some difficulty in getting your dog to respond to the dumbbell, this is only normal and is nothing for you to become distressed about. Some of these reluctant fellows turn out to be the best and happiest "retrievers" after proper training.

Part Three

Let us continue with another phase of dumbbell work. We will begin teaching the dog to pick the dumbbell from the ground.

Be sure, before starting this particular portion of the exercise, that your dog is successfully performing the procedure of reaching for the dumbbell.

To begin with in this part of the training, you need not be too particular about the position of your dog. It is not necessary that he remain in the heel position at the beginning. Make sure, however, that the lead and choke chain are on the dog in the proper manner. One other thing you should do before starting each day's lesson is refresh the dog by having him take and reach for the dumbbell a couple of times.

The first thing to do is find a clean, level surface to work on. The type of surface is not important, but the height is. You can work inside or out—it makes no difference—but the object you use to put the dumbbell on should be just slightly lower than the dog's mouth. This may sound somewhat eccentric, but you will find that getting the dog to take the dumbbell from a surface is a rather ominous experience for your dog and you will want to give him every advantage while training. If you do not have anything that is the proper height for your particular dog, then make your own by using a stack of books. This is my preference because they are adjustable, which is a necessity as your dog progresses.

After you have chosen the surface you wish to use, simply place your dumbbell on top of it. Bring your dog to a position directly in front of the dumbbell, saying *take* as many times as necessary to encourage him to reach for the dumbbell. Once the dumbbell is in his mouth, respond with the word *hold* immediately. Do not allow the dog to drop the dumbbell! Insist that the dog hold it for a few seconds. Then, using the command *out*, remove the dumbbell from the dog's mouth.

When you find that you are successful with this procedure, begin lowering the surface gradually. If you have used books, as suggested, remove several books and try the exercise again. Continue this procedure until the dog is taking the dumb-

With the dumbbell on the ground, use as many take *commands as necessary to obtain a favorable response from the dog.*

bell from the ground. Once this is accomplished, then you are ready to experiment with different surfaces such as grass, cement, wood, or carpet. The one important factor to remember when doing this, however, is that you place the dumbbell a distance away from him.

This exercise appears to be very simple but it's really quite deceptive. It is easier for the handler than for the dog; this you must remember. Do not overtire your dog or push him beyond his capacity when working with this exercise. It is certainly not expected that you will accomplish this entire procedure in one day. Do as much as possible and begin where you left off the next day.

There is one very common problem in this phase of the

Do not become distressed if the dog lays down, putting his head on the dumbbell.

training that you will undoubtedly encounter: Your dog will probably lay his head on the dumbbell instead of picking it up. This is to be expected; simply remove the dumbbell gently from under his chin, put it back in place, and start over.

Another problem with this exercise is that no matter how perfectly your dog has been reaching for the dumbbell from your hand, he will refuse to take it from the surface at first. You should assist him by encouraging him to move toward it and also by lifting a portion of the dumbbell from the surface for him. When he takes it, then praise him abundantly. The only thing to remember about giving praise when working with the dumbbell is that you must not excite the dog and cause him to goof. Be abundant with your appreciation but not exhuberant.

The Final Stage

As opposed to the procedure followed in part three, you will start by being particular about the position of the dog. Be sure that he is sitting in the correct heel position. Have his lead properly attached to his collar, and do not hold the lead; allow it to dangle on the ground. Be sure that the lead is neatly placed so that the dog will not trip over it but will also be easily accessible to you.

It would be advantageous to do this portion of the training in a confined area such as your garage or basement. In other words, the dog should not have a lot of room to roam. With the dog sitting correctly at your left side, command him to *stay*, then throw the dumbbell approximately two feet in front of you. Command the dog to *take* and simultaneously make a sweeping motion with your left hand toward the dumbbell. Excitedly repeat the command *take* several times. At the exact moment the dog shows an interest in going after the dumbbell, encourage him by giving verbal praise such as *good boy*. As soon as he picks the dumbbell from the ground into his mouth, give the command *hold*. Then, immediately pick up the lead and start backpedaling while you are giving the command to *come*. Keep backing up about ten feet, until the dog is in front of you with the dumbbell in his mouth, then command him to *sit*. Be sure that the dog does not drop the dumbbell. Then reach for the dumbbell, commanding distinctly *out*. Remove the dumbbell with both hands. Obviously, you must throw the lead over your shoulder before giving the out command so that your hands are free to work with the dumbbell.

If you have any problem in getting the dog to release the

Begin with the dog sitting correctly at your left side.

Throw the dumbbell directly forward only a few feet.

dumbbell, use the procedure that you used previously when teaching the dog to take the dumbbell, which is opening his mouth yourself and removing the dumbbell. Another difficulty that you may encounter in this first portion of the final stage is that your dog may refuse to sit when returning to you with the dumbbell. Simply reach past him and gently press on his hindquarters, reminding him to sit. Perhaps it seems impossible to you that your dog could ignore a command he knows so well by this time, such as *sit*, but you must remember that he is concentrating on holding that dumbbell in his mouth and this entire procedure is new and he is not sure of himself as yet.

Once you are successful with the retrieval at this distance, then progress to a distance of about six feet—a full lead length. Repeat the entire procedure that you used previously. Be sure that while you are working with the lead you never allow it to tighten. This could easily be misunderstood as a reprimand by the dog. Since the dumbbell is a reasonable distance away from you for the first time, your dog may be reluctant to leave you and go after it. Encourage him by accompanying him part of the way along with your verbal commands. Then drop back, allow him to continue by himself. Eventually he will understand that leaving your side is permitted and will do so willingly. You must keep in mind that this also is an entirely new experience for the dog.

Having had success with your on lead retrieves, you are ready for the big step: working off lead with the dumbbell. You will simply remove the lead from the dog's collar. Then, using exactly the same procedure described previously, throw the dumbbell about six feet to start with. Remember to repeat the verbal commands as many times as you deem necessary. The dog's mind must be kept busy, and this can be done by giving continuous proper commands. Since he is off lead and is expected to retrieve an article and return it

When the dog reaches the dumbbell, immediately command take.

to you, his thoughts must be controlled by you, otherwise he will become interested in something else and forget completely what he is to accomplish. Continue this procedure, gradually increasing the distance until your dog will retrieve the dumbbell from the maximum distance of 30 feet.

When working with your dog off lead, you may find that he will anticipate going after the dumbbell. If this happens to you, simply take advantage of the situation and encourage him. When your dog retrieves the dumbbell, if he shows any indication that he might not return to you, start praising him verbally and clap your hands in an excited manner. He will understand that you are pleased and you will have diverted his attention from any interference.

After your dog becomes proficient in retrieving the dumbbell, then you must eliminate any anticipation along with all extra commands. The dog will be told *stay*, then *take*. He will retrieve the dumbbell and you will not say another word until after he sits in front of you. Then command *out* and finally command *heel*, at which time he will return to the heel position. This is what you are striving for. It will not happen overnight.

Require the dog to sit directly in front of you, still holding the dumbbell.

Using both hands, command the dog out *and remove the dumbbell from his mouth.*

Each individual and his dog are different. There is no average time allotment for this exercise. The object is to obtain perfection, not see how fast you can accomplish the lessons. Once your dog has learned to retrieve and carry an object, you can have a lot of fun by allowing him to carry the newspaper or a pair of slippers and many other objects for which retrieving is the basis.

You will find that having done your part well, your dog will enjoy retrieving. Although this particular exercise is difficult and requires a great deal of work and patience on your part, there is nothing to match that moment when your dog retrieves perfectly and bounces into you, sitting there with an object in his mouth and a look on his face that tells you, "Well, here it is. What do you want me to do with it?"

14
The Jump

Part One

TEACHING YOUR DOG TO JUMP ON COMMAND SUCCESSFULLY will depend a great deal on how efficiently you execute the basic steps involved in laying the foundation for this exercise.

The first thing you must do is to obtain or construct the proper equipment. For those of you who now or intend to participate in American Kennel Club Obedience Trials, I recommend that you obtain regulation jumps of which there are two: the solid jump and the bar jump. Specifications for regulation jumps are outlined in detail in the appendix.

At the beginning, no matter what breed you have, place the jump only eight inches from the ground. The object of this first experience is simply to teach the dog the meaning of the command *jump*. Start with the dog on lead, about 10 feet away from the jump. Have him sitting in the proper heel position facing the center of the jump.

Hold the bulk of the lead in your right hand and guide the remainder of the lead with the left hand. Be sure to keep a loose lead at all times. Approach the jump with the dog at

Approach the jump at a reasonable rate of speed for your particular dog.

a reasonable rate of speed for your individual dog, and just as you reach the obstacle command the dog to *jump* and simultaneously give a quick snap of the lead to project the dog over the jump. You are, of course, jumping with the dog. After clearing the jump, praise the dog enthusiastically. Do not worry about the position of the dog at this point. Repeat this procedure as many times as is feasible, but keep in mind that warm or humid weather can be a determining factor, as this is a very strenuous endeavor for your dog.

It might be better to practice early in the morning or late in the evening. Do not feed your dog before jumping him.

After performing this step a few times, try leaving your dog on one side of the jump and standing opposite him on the other side of the jump. Simply call your dog, and just as

Command the dog to jump, *then go over the obstacle with him.*

he approaches the obstacle, command *jump*, bringing him to a sit directly in front of you. Practice jumping the dog in both directions.

Be sure that your dog is actually jumping. Some of the larger breeds will easily clear eight inches by walking over it. Do not allow this. This can be avoided by maintaining a happy attitude yourself and giving a lot of encouragement to the dog just as he approaches the jump. Under no circumstances should you allow your dog to jump any higher than the recommended eight inches during the first session.

A word of caution for those of you who happen to own a dog that is physically impaired in any way or whose dog is very old: This exercise is not advocated. If you have any doubts, please use your own good judgment or consult your veterinarian.

Keep your eyes and ears open for opportunities to use the word *jump* around the house during your daily activities. Any time your dog leaps onto something, command him to *jump*. This will inadvertently help teach him the meaning of the word.

Part Two

The first thing that you must do before going any further with the jumping lesson is to measure the height of your dog. Just simply use any type of measuring device and determine how high your dog stands at the withers. When referring to the height of your dog at any time in the instructions, this is the height to which I am referring.

Any healthy dog, no matter what the breed, is capable of jumping, which is why you will begin the jumping exercise using this measurement. To determine how high your dog will eventually jump, the American Kennel Club has made recommendations to be used in obedience trial competition, and I am sure this is the most reliable source you can refer to.

These recommendations are that small dogs such as Basset Hounds, Dachshunds, Corgis, Clumber and Sussex Spaniels, Maltese, Pekingese, Bulldogs, French Bulldogs and almost all terriers should always jump the height of the dog or eight inches, whichever is greater.

The same rule applies to large, heavy breeds, such as Bloodhounds, Bullmastiffs, Great Danes, Great Pyrenees, Mastiffs, Newfoundlands, and St. Bernards. These breeds will again jump only their height at the withers or 36 inches, whichever is less.

The remainder of the breeds, not named specifically, will jump one and one-half times their height at the withers but never higher than 36 inches. Some specific breeds in this category are the German Shepherd, Irish Setter, Golden Retriever, Brittany Spaniel or Shetland Sheepdog, Poodles, etc.

If you are the owner of a mixed breed dog, be sure to use the recommendations for the breed he most resembles in structure and weight for determination of the height that he should jump.

After studying the height instructions, if you have a dog that can jump higher than the eight inches you have already attempted, you are ready to try raising the jump a little higher. For now, you should only raise the jump to about half the distance the dog will finally jump according to the standards previously stated.

Begin your daily sessions by reviewing the original eight inches and refreshing your dog's memory to the command

As you are helping the dog project himself over the jump, be sure to hold the lead high enough to clear the verticle end of the obstacle.

jump. Practice this a couple of times, then raise your jump. Obviously, the jump is getting a little high for some of you to be able to jump with the dog.

With your dog on lead, run with the dog at a brisk pace until you are about two feet from the jump. Then in an enthusiastic tone of voice, command the dog to *jump*, simultaneously helping the dog over the jump. At this exact point, you the handler must step aside to a position parallel to the jump. Be sure that your lead is held high enough to clear the vertical end of the jump.

Take advantage of the entire six feet of your lead when performing this exercise. You must be careful, when allowing the dog to jump with the lead on, that you do not tighten the lead in any way and that you never get the lead tangled on the jump. If you incorrectly handle your lead, the safest thing to do is release it immediately, allowing the dog free movement.

Part Three

This third phase of the jumping exercise will consist of working with the dog off lead.

Still maintaining the jump at a height that is only about half the height your dog is capable of jumping, position youself and your dog about five feet from the jump. Using a method similar to the one previously employed during the on-lead work, advance with the dog at a brisk pace toward the jump, and with your left hand give a directive motion toward the jump along with the command *jump*. Allow the dog to complete the jump alone, and you will therefore find yourself on the opposite side of the jump from the dog. At this point, command the dog to *come* and simultaneously encourage him to return over the jump to you by continuing to call him and tapping the top of the jump with your hand.

Advance with the dog at a brisk pace toward the jump, giving a directive motion with your left arm.

Encourage the dog to return over the jump by tapping the top of the jump and commanding come *simultaneously.*

Again, as the dog approaches the jump, be sure to give the command *jump* then back up quickly to avoid the dog bumping into you and require him to sit in front of you.

As you can see, the basic lesson seems relatively simple. However, the most important phase of this exercise is the development of precise timing and absolute communication between you and your dog.

Let us, at this point, discuss some of the problems most often encountered. One of them will be hesitation. Your dog will approach the jump, but will pause and become hesitant about jumping. Do not force him to continue at this point; return to the original distance and start forward again. If the same thing happens, put the dog on lead and help him over the jump with a smart snap of the lead, using the command *jump*. Carefully handling the lead, bring him back over the jump to you in the same manner. After you have done this, remove the lead and try the new exercise again. Generally, hesitation is caused by simply being a little off in your timing and practice will correct this.

Perhaps the most perplexing occurrence of this exercise is that the dog will attempt to go around the jump rather than over it. If your dog at any time decides to avoid the jump, give a firm command of *no* and prevent him from doing so. Then take the dog back to the beginning and start all over again. It is not uncommon for this to happen several times. Therefore, do not become distressed if it happens to you. One of the causes of this problem is often the fact that the dog is insecure because he has not sufficiently learned the meaning of the word *jump*. If this happens consistently, the only solution is to go back to the beginning lesson and teach the dog again.

Another difficulty with this exercise is the same as in any off-lead work: You must keep the dog's attention at all times. For example, when the dog leaves your side and goes over the jump, just as he touches the ground on the other side, distinctly call his name to obtain his attention and then immediately respond with your *come* command to bring him back over the jump to you.

At this point, you are probably thinking that this exercise is nothing but one problem after another. However, these particular difficulties are almost synonymous with the process of teaching your dog to jump.

So, "chin up" and remember my favorite word—patience. There is still a long way to go to perfect the jumping exercise, but as with anything worthwhile, you can't expect to accomplish it without a little hard work!

Part Four

You are now beginning the fourth stage of teaching your dog to jump the high hurdle. Therefore, it is now time to attempt to jump the dog and have him retrieve the dumbbell.

If your training has progressed reasonably well, then the dog should definitely know the meaning of the command *jump* by this time. What remains is simply a matter of methodically "putting it all together."

Begin this phase by keeping the jump at no less than eight inches and no more than half the distance your dog will eventually jump, depending upon the individual breed and the agility with which the dog clears the jump.

This exercise is called "retrieve over the high jump." The first question that will probably enter your mind is, why not finish jumping the dog to his fullest capacity before starting something new? The reason for this is that your dog must learn to combine the two exercises before he can possibly be expected to achieve a maximum high jump along with carrying the dumbbell in his mouth.

You will start this procedure by putting your dog back on

lead. Then, with your dog in the proper heel position, stand a reasonably short distance from the high jump. Holding the dumbbell in your right hand and the lead in your left hand, gently toss the dumbbell just on the other side of the jump.

Just as you have been doing for the past few lessons, approach the jump with your dog commanding him to *jump* as he reaches the hurdle. After he has completed the jump, immediately command *take*. Use as many commands as necessary to get the dog to take the dumbbell from the ground and as soon as he has the dumbbell firmly in his mouth, with the lead still in your hand, command him to *jump* again. You will not go over the obstacle with him, but remain in your original position and allow the dog to return to you. Once the dog is sitting in front of you with the dumbbell in his mouth, reach for the dumbbell using the command *out*, remove the dumbbell from his mouth.

I think you can easily see now why it is advisable not to have the jump set too high. You must have a great deal of mobility to properly maneuver the dog and yourself. It is imperative that you do not allow the dog to become tangled in his lead and above all be very careful that he does not bump into the jump with the dumbbell in his mouth. Most importantly, your dog could injure his mouth or teeth, but you could also create a problem that would be very difficult to correct.

A reasonable amount of difficulty is expected with a new exercise and it is especially true when you are attempting to combine two procedures for the first time. However, if you seem to be having more than the average amount of problems, simply stop and analyze the situation. You might find that you need further practice in one particular area or perhaps both. If this happens to be the case, then start with one at a time and perfect each one before trying the combination again.

Again, the most important fact for you as a handler to remember is proper timing in giving commands and praise. Be sure that your commands are firm, but not menacing. You must time your commands so that the proper ones are given at the exact moment they are needed. Your praise must be immediate. For example, the instant your dog retrieves the dumbbell, tell him *good boy* and follow up quickly with the command *jump*.

It would be advantageous for you to read the directions for the exercise several times before attempting to execute them. If you know without a doubt what you want to accomplish, you can concentrate on performing the exercise without having to try to remember what comes next. If you have had any problems with timing your commands, this

Command the dog to stay *and throw the dumbbell over the jump.*

Remaining in your original position, command the dog to jump.

The dog must retrieve the dumbbell and return over the jump *without hesitation.*

could be one of the reasons. You cannot possibly be expected to have to stop and think what to do and still be able to get proper timing into your work.

Part Five

This phase of the training will consist of teaching the dog to jump over the solid jump and retrieve the dumbbell—off lead.

Keeping the jump at the same height you have been working with thus far, start by positioning yourself and the dog the same distance from the jump that you were using in performing your on-lead work. The only difference is that you will now remove the lead.

Holding the dumbbell in your right hand, give the command and hand signal (with your left hand) to *stay*. Then, gently throw the dumbbell over the jump, placing it as nearly as possible in the middle. Leading with your left foot, take one step forward and make a sweeping motion towards the jump with your left hand, simultaneously giving the command *jump* in a clear but jubilant tone of voice.

As soon as the dog makes contact with the ground on the other side of the obstacle, command the dog to *take*. Then as the dog takes the dumbbell into his mouth, immediately command the dog *jump*, thus bringing him back over the obstacle. When he completes the return jump and comes to you, give the command *sit*. Keep the dog sitting in front of you, and take the dumbbell from his mouth giving him the command *out*.

If your dog fails to respond to the first command to jump, then run with the dog to the obstacle. At the exact point you reach the jump together, apply the sweeping hand motion described previously and give several verbal commands to *jump*.

Holding the dumbbell in your left hand, give the command and hand signal (with your left hand) to stay.

Assuming you may have a problem with the dog refusing to pick up the dumbbell once he has taken the jump, you must go around the jump to the dog, point to the dumbbell, and with a firm tone of voice command the dog *take*. If he still refuses to respond, the only solution is to take the choke collar and gently pull him to the dumbbell giving the command *take*. The instant the dog takes the dumbbell, you must quickly return to your original position on the other side of the hurdle in time to give the dog the command to *jump* without allowing him to come around it. One of the most important factors for you as a trainer to remember concerning this portion of the exercise is that you must never allow the dog to return over the obstacle without retrieving the dumbbell.

The instant the dog retrieves the dumbbell, command jump *to prevent the temptation of going around the obstacle.*

Some of you will develop a different type of problem because the dog is working off lead in this exercise for the first time: the dog will attempt to return to you without jumping over the obstacle. In other words, he will go around the jump rather than over it. You most definitely must prevent this. If you are working alone, it can be done by commanding *no* in a firm tone of voice. This will usually stop the dog from moving. Go to the dog on the other side of the jump and take him back a few feet from the obstacle; give him the command to *stay*. You then return to your original position on the other side of the jump and call your dog using the command *come*, until he reaches the obstacle, then command *jump*.

If you have a dog that consistently persists in attempting

to go around the jump, try to get one or more persons to work with you. Position them on each side of the jump, standing directly parallel with the obstacle. In this case, if the dog attempts to go around the jump, have your helper take a step toward the dog to block him; you should quickly get the dog's attention, commanding him to *jump*.

If your dog is taking the original jump, retrieving the dumbbell, and approaching the obstacle to jump but seems confused or hesitant, then without delay run up to the jump and, with your hands, tap the top of the obstacle, giving the command *jump*. As soon as he responds, back up to give him room to complete the jump.

The Final Stage

If your dog has performed the lessons proficiently thus far, then it is time to raise the jump to the full height that your individual dog is capable of. To begin this lesson, practice with the jump set at the height with which you have been working thus far. Then as the dog progresses, gradually raise the jump until you have reached the maximum height. Be sure that each time you raise the jump the dog continues to perform all phases of retrieving correctly. This is just as important as actually being able to clear the obstacle.

The only commands that are necessary (or allowed in competition) in enacting this exercise are as follows: Standing with your dog off lead in the heel position, with your left hand tell the dog *stay*. Then throw the dumbbell, giving the command *jump*. After the dog returns to you with the dumbbell, command him *out* as you remove the dumbbell from his mouth. Obviously, there are only three permissible verbal commands. Instead of using the verbal command *jump* you may use the sweeping hand motion if you find it more effective. But remember, this can be used only instead

Raise the level gradually until your dog can jump the height required of him as efficiently as Lancer does here.

of the verbal command, not along with it.

If you begin having problems with a dog that is not responding without using extra commands, then gradually eliminate them, one by one, until only the three permissible commands are being used.

You will probably find praise a very advantageous asset in helping to eliminate the actual commands. Logically, the dog is going to be confused at first by your lack of verbal communication with him. Your silence will undoubtedly cause him to hesitate and seem dubious about what to do. So you must compensate temporarily with something and what could be better than what he wants to hear—praise. Once you have the dog reassured that he is doing what is

At this stage in the training procedure, the dog should be able to perform the entire exercise without extra physical or verbal commands.

expected of him, then you can gradually eliminate the praise until the exercise is completed.

During previous training, it was recommended that you remain in a position that gave you immediate access to your dog in case a correction was necessary. By this time, you should be ready to maintain a position that gives you a more logical perspective of the obstacle. This will be determined by the breed of dog with which you are working and his agility.

Another item that you will want to take into consideration at this time is the distance you have been throwing the dumbbell. So far, the dumbbell has been kept in a position giving the dog every advantage. To accomplish your ultimate goal of having a good retriever, you will want to start throwing the dumbbell a further distance. This too, must be done gradually. Your best guide here is your own judgment. Know your dog and his particular capabilities. For those of you who are planning on showing your dog in American Kennel Club competition, you should practice throwing your dumbbell a little to the left and to the right. This is in the event that inadvertently this would happen to you in a show. You would not be caught by surprise, but would have a dog that could retrieve the dumbbell, regardless of the position where it lands.

There is another perplexing experience that you could encounter, which I wish to discuss with you at this point. Since you are going to be working with the jump at a greater height than in the past, there is the remote possibility that the dog might accidentally bump into the jump. This is something that I certainly hope you will make every effort to avoid, but in the event that it should happen, you must know what to do. Simply forget everything else, go to your dog, and, in a calm, soothing manner, praise him. After checking your dog to make sure that he is not physically injured in any way, determine what caused this to happen. If you deem it necessary, lower your hurdle and require him to perform the exercise again. If the dog jumps again as soon as possible, he will not develop a mental shyness of the obstacle because of his unfortunate experience.

The Bar Jump

There are two major differences between the "bar jump" and the "solid jump." The first is that the dog will not be required to retrieve the dumbbell when performing the bar jump and the second is that the dog may attempt to go under the bar rather than over it.

Using your own good judgment, be aware of your own dog's restrictions such as weight, height, and physical fitness to create a happy, well-adjusted worker.

Dorian illustrates a perfectly executed retrieve over the high jump.

If this occurs, you must again exercise the word *no* in a firm tone of voice. Your objective is to stop the dog immediately. Then use the same procedure described previously for prevention of allowing the dog to go around the solid jump. There is also an alternative suggestion: When you are using the bar and the dog persists on trying to go under it, lower it to a position that makes it almost impossible for him to get under. Raise it gradually as he becomes proficient in performing the exercise.

Don't forget to take advantage of your efforts in obedience training your dog in your everyday activities. Now that he has learned to jump, you will find that getting the dog into the family automobile is a lot easier, especially for those of you with extra large breeds. If you are walking your dog in the rain and you see an upcoming puddle, simply command him to jump instead of walking through the water. The same would apply to a situation where your dog would place himself somewhere off the ground he shouldn't be, simply tell him to jump instead of tugging at him to get him down.

15
Broad Jump

THE BROAD JUMP CONSISTS OF FOUR HURDLES THAT TELESCOPE. It should be a total of five feet in length, with each board about eight inches in width. At the highest point, it should only be about six inches high. These should be painted a flat white.

Remembering the specifications given for determining the height your dog would jump over the high jump, use those same measurements to determine the length your dog will jump over the broad jump. Simply take the height required for your specific breed and multiply by two. In other words, if your dog jumped the maximum of 36 inches over the high jump, then his broad jump at maximum distance would be 72 inches. By the way, 72 inches is the maximum distance for any breed of dog for the broad jump. The minimum distance required is 16 inches.

When arranging the broad jump in preparation for jumping your dog, it should be set up according to the graduation of height of the boards. You will jump your dog from the lowest point. You should stand no further than 10 feet back from the jump; however, you may stand as close as you wish.

You will determine how many boards to use for your breed of dog by the number of inches he is required to jump. For example, if your dog jumps from 52" to 72" use four boards; from 32" to 48" use three boards; from 16" to 28" use two boards. Place them always an equal distance apart. This way you will note that there is always some space between each board. Be sure to measure your distance as a total of the boards and the spaces in between.

Start this exercise with your dog on lead in the proper heel position. In this lesson, as in all jumping exercises, do not start with all of the boards. If you have a small breed, use only one board in the beginning. For the larger breeds, you may begin with two. Approach the hurdle with your

Stand with your dog, in the heel position, at a reasonable distance from the broad jump.

Approach the broad jump with the dog, commanding jump *and maintaining a loose lead.*

As soon as the dog completes the jump, bring him to the correct front position.

dog and give the command *jump*; be sure to keep pace with your dog, maintaining a loose lead at all times. The minute the dog's feet touch the ground, using the command *come*, bring the dog into the front position. After the dog is sitting in front of you, give the command *heel*, thereby ending the exercise with the dog in the proper heel position. When you bring the dog to the front position alongside the broad jump, you should be standing about two feet away from the hurdles. Be very conscientious about this, because you must not be any further than two feet away from the hurdles, but you will want to be sure to use the full distance allowed so that your dog has room to properly heel.

After you and the dog clear the hurdles several times, tell your dog to *stay*. Walk to a spot in the middle of the one or two hurdles, whichever you are using at this point, and give the command *jump*. Again, bring the dog to the front position and finish with *heel*. When performing this portion of the exercise, you must be very careful that you do not allow the lead to tighten.

Since your dog already knows the jump command, you will probably not have any problem with his responding to the actual command, however there will be some other problems that could develop. Perhaps the most common of these is that now, and later when you are using more than one board, your dog will try to walk between the boards rather than jump over them. Another factor that you must watch for, even at the beginning when you are still working with the dog on lead, is the cutting of corners. Make sure that he always jumps over the middle of the hurdles. This is one of the reasons that you must not allow the lead to tighten, because you could cause this problem to manifest itself through your own carelessness.

One solution for the dog that persists in walking through the jumps is to stand alongside the hurdle, placing one foot inside between the boards. Then, as you give the command *jump*, quickly snap the lead helping the dog project himself over the hurdles. You will be encouraging him to clear the hurdle rather than walking through it because your foot will be in his way.

The word *come*, which you are using to teach the dog what to do the instant he lands, is an extra command, but please use it only until your dog turns automatically and comes to you without being called.

In the beginning, keep your dog on lead and use only one or two hurdles. Be sure to use any commands that are necessary when teaching a new exercise to keep the dog's attention and keep him busy doing what he is being instructed to do. Don't be a spectator standing there waiting to see what is going to happen next. This is one of the secrets of becoming a good trainer.

Broad Jump—Off Lead

Assuming that you have been successful thus far, you will begin this phase of the training by adding the additional boards necessary to obtain the maximum jump for your particular breed of dog. You will start with your dog still on lead.

Commencing with the dog in the proper heel position, continue to perform the exercise in the same manner you have been using—the only difference being that you have added the additional boards, thus requiring him to jump a further distance.

Repeat this portion of the exercise several times, remembering to keep pace with your dog as he clears the jump and bring him to the proper front position. Then finish as usual by commanding the dog to the correct heel position.

Something new you should add to your training while the

dog is still on lead is a hand signal. Holding the lead in your right hand, use your left hand and arm to give a sweeping motion across the jump simultaneously commanding the dog to *jump*. This will be a most effective asset when you start working off lead.

Once you determine that your dog is performing this exercise on lead without hesitation and without any problems, take the lead off. Now you must be absolutely sure that your timing is as nearly perfect as possible. Using all the extra commands recommended and the hand signal, try your dog off lead with all the boards. If you find that you are having no problems, then tell the dog to *stay*, position yourself properly alongside the broad jump, and command

Place your foot slightly inside the boards and, using the hand signal, command the dog to jump.

the dog to *jump*. It is advisable to still use the extra commands at this point. Only after the dog jumps several times successfully with all the extra commands can you begin to eliminate them.

The only commands that you will use when you conclude that the dog no longer needs extra help are the hand signal and command to *stay*. Then use either the hand signal or voice command to *jump* and complete the exercise by commanding the dog to *heel*.

It will not be at all unusual for some dogs that have been working perfectly on lead to suddenly start having problems off lead. The dog may start walking through the jump at this point, even if he has not done so before. If this happens put the dog back on lead, then take one of the boards and place it on end in an upright position. With the dog still on lead, complete the exercise several times with the board in this position. Then quickly remove the lead, with the board still in the upright position, and command the dog to *jump*.

After the dog stops walking through the jump, place the board back into the proper position. Because your dog has been taught to jump over a high hurdle, this will in a small way seem similar and therefore be the incentive for him to jump rather than walk.

Since your dog is working off lead and is no longer being guided over the jump, he may decide to start "cutting the corner." This too, can be corrected by altering your initial heel position. Simply start with the dog facing slightly to the left. Therefore, as the dog jumps, even if he has a tendency to veer to the right, he will still be in the center of the jump. Use this method only as long as necessary, do not make it a habit.

Again, a word of caution to all handlers. Don't be in a hurry to exercise your dog off lead. I know that this is always a temptation. It is only natural to be anxious to see what he

To prevent "walking" through the boards, place the first board upright, thus simulating in a small way the previously learned high jump.

will do without the lead, but you will only create problems that need not ever exist if you rush when teaching the dog a new exercise. This exercise is not a difficult one, but you will make it difficult if you do not have patience.

Most of you will probably find that a quick review of each new lesson is always helpful at the beginning of each practice session. Even if your dog is working reasonably well off lead, a couple of on-lead jumps at the start will help him progress faster in the long run.

Most importantly, don't forget that praise! Sometimes, as we progress further into obedience work, we take our dog's capabilities for granted. This is a tremendous mistake. He is constantly learning something new and must be encouraged every step of the way. Remember that through cooperating with you and constantly trying to please you while performing these exercises, he is showing his devotion to you. So don't become complacent, but praise him immediately for a job well done and show him how much affection and respect you have for him as well.

16
Scent Discrimination

THE PURPOSE OF SCENT DISCRIMINATION IS TO TEACH THE DOG to select from a group of articles the one that has been handled by you, using scent alone. He must then retrieve it and bring the article to you.

The first thing that you must do is obtain the proper articles. You will need a total of 10. Five should be made of leather and five should be of metal. Each set must match identically, and cannot be more than six inches in length. The metal set must be made entirely of rigid metal. The leather set must be made entirely of leather with the exception that they may be held together by a minimum amount of thread or metal necessary for this purpose.

For anyone who wishes a professionally made set of articles, they can be purchased through your local pet store or by ordering from a pet supply catalog. If you want to make your own articles, you can use many everyday items. One of the simplest metal articles to make is from jar rings. Select jar rings of medium size and solder one-half of a jar ring to the top of a whole jar ring, giving the impression of a handle. You can use tin snips to cut the rings into halves.

There are a total of ten articles, five leather and five metal.

To make the leather set you can use strips of leather about one inch wide, such as purse straps or leather belts. You can also purchase leather for this purpose at very little expense. Just cut the leather in equal size pieces, making sure that you remember the articles should not exceed six inches in length when completed. Once the leather is cut into pieces, then just place the two ends together and hold with a rivet or glue.

The next step is to number each set of articles from one through five. Again, you can purchase small stick-on numbers for this purpose, or, if you prefer, you can simply use nail enamel. Then add a pair of kitchen tongs to your sets of articles. You may want to obtain some sort of adequate carrying case for this equipment.

SCENT DISCRIMINATION / 147

To start the training for this particular exercise, take one of the metal articles and throw it about six feet in front of you. Using the retrieve command *take*, send your dog to retrieve the articles. Repeat this a few times until your dog takes the metal article without hesitation. The purpose for this is so that your dog gets the feel of carrying metal in his mouth.

The next step is to take another metal article, and using the tongs, place it about six feet from you. You must be very careful not to touch this particular article with any part of your body, not even your finger. Then take the article that the dog has been retrieving and rub it thoroughly with your hands, thereby placing your scent on its entirety. Gently toss the article you have scented about six inches away from the article already placed in front of you. Then, place your left hand directly in front of the dog's nose, allowing him to sniff your hand. This is giving him the scent.

Again, with the dog off lead, command him to retrieve the article. You will, of course, want him to retrieve only the one that is scented.

As the dog reaches the two articles, he will probably become confused and you must then "talk" him onto the correct article. This will be done by clearly, but in a gentle tone of voice, giving an additional command *get it*.

If he approaches the wrong article, calmly command him *no* using an elongated tone. When he approaches the correct article, encourage him, still using a calm voice by telling him *good boy*. When he picks up the correct article, call him to you in the front position with the article in his mouth. Then, using the command *out*, remove the article from his mouth. Praise him jubilantly,

Preferably this exercise should be started with the dog off lead, so that you can concentrate on giving commands to help him select the proper article. However, if he refuses to work off lead, then you must put him on lead. Obviously, this lesson is better executed in a confined area. This will prevent the dog from wandering off without putting him on lead.

This exercise is one that demands careful instruction on your part. It is absolutely necessary that you understand what you want to accomplish before starting to work with your dog. Above all, do not become impatient. Do not try to progress beyond these few simple steps, until they are perfected. You will find that this exercise cannot b rushed.

Repeat the verbal commands as many times as necessary to get the dog to pick up the scented article. If he sniffs the wrong article but makes no attempt to take it in his mouth, then allow him to do this. Actually, this is what you are trying to accomplish. You want him to sniff both articles but retrieve only the one with the scent you have given him.

The Second Stage

Assuming that you have been successful thus far, you are now ready for the next step in scent discrimination.

Instead of tossing the scented article near the article that is already placed about six feet in front of you, take the scented article and place it near the one already there. You are still working with just the metal articles. You are, of course, remembering not to touch any articles that you do not want the dog to retrieve. You must use tongs to put these unscented articles in their place.

You will then stand with your dog in the proper heel position, but with your back toward the articles. This is the position that you will always use from now on when performing this exercise. Give the dog your scent with your left hand. As soon as you have done this, turn with your dog toward the articles simultaneously giving him the command *get it*.

If you are working alone and have to place the scented article yourself, give your dog the command to *stay*. Do not allow him to accompany you while you are performing this function. If it is possible to have someone assist you with this exercise, then allow your assistant to place the scented article with the tongs in its proper place and you remain with the dog.

As soon as your dog is properly discriminating the scented article from the other metal article, you are ready to add still another article to the group. As long as you are successful, continue to add the remainder of the metal articles one by one. It is advisable to keep them in a group, but a reasonable distance apart for the present time. Do not make a particular design with the articles; allow them to be placed at random, not scattered carelessly.

If you proceed with this phase of the exercise without pushing your dog beyond his capabilities, then by the time all the metal articles are employed your dog will have no problem distinguishing the scented article from the group of five.

Once the dog scents the metal faultlessly, you are ready to begin the leather. You will remove all the metal articles and work only with the leather. Again, start with just two articles and continue working until you have no problem working with five. You may find that the dog adapts more readily to the leather than he did the metal. However, don't be surprised if some of the same problems appear that you experienced when first beginning with the metal. The reason is that you have changed materials, and the dog is still very inexperienced with the scenting procedure.

After each training session, place the articles not touching each other in a place where they can be aired. This is to

To give the dog the scent, place your hand directly in front of the dog's nose, allowing him to sniff your hand.

Allow the dog to scent at his own discretion, as long as he does not attempt to pick up the wrong article.

allow your scent to disappear from the article you have touched. There is no harm done if someone else touches the articles. In fact, this is most desirable. (With the exception of the scented article when you are working the dog.) Do not scent the same article today that you used yesterday. For the simple reason that the dog could begin to choose the scented article by some means other than smelling it.

Keep in mind, as mentioned previously, that the dog should be allowed to smell any article in the group as long as he does not attempt to pick it up. In the event the dog would pick up the wrong article before you can prevent it, give him the command *out*. Hopefully he will automatically drop the article. If he does not, then you must remove the

As soon as the dog obtains the correct article, encourage him to bring it directly to you.

article with your hands and put it aside for the rest of the training session. You cannot put it back with the group because you have just scented that particular article by touching it.

If you see the dog hovers over the scented article, but hesitates to pick it up, calmly walk to him and point to the article, telling him to *get it*. When he responds, quickly praise him verbally as you back up to your original position while instructing the dog to come to the front position.

Final Stage

Thus far, you have been working with the leather articles and the metal articles separately. Now, let's combine the two sets.

Begin by using only one leather article and one metal article. Place the leather article the proper distance away with the tongs. Then with your dog in the correct heel position and your back toward the article, scent the metal article. Place the scented metal article about six inches away from the unscented leather article. Give your dog the scent and command him to *get it*.

Once the dog successfully retrieves the scented metal article, simply reverse the situation. If the dog progresses favorably with this opposite procedure, gradually add the remaining articles one by one until you attain the maximum amount of articles. Remember to keep one leather and one metal article for scenting purposes, therefore you will eventually have eight unscented articles.

Make sure, when placing the unscented articles in their respective area that you allow about six inches space between each article. Never allow them to touch each other.

If, at any time, the dog seems to regress, revert to a lesser number of articles. Do not hesitate to do this. Be very observant when working with your dog so that you are able to determine any problem he is encountering. More often than not, it will simply be a case of trying to progress faster than his capabilities will allow.

Be prepared, when working with the maximum amount of articles, to permit the dog ample time to scent the articles. As long as the dog is obviously working, he is allowed to use an adequate amount of time. You will know immediately when he is not applying himself to the project when he starts to wander away or continuously looks around without making any gesture toward the articles.

So far, you have been encouraged to use any verbal commands necessary to accomplish your purpose. When you feel the dog is scenting with confidence, begin to eliminate the extra commands. This exercise permits the giving of the scent with your left hand; then turn and give the command *get it*. You will remain motionless and silent until the dog returns to you with the correct article, then command *out* and finish with the *heel* command. He will be required to scent one metal and one leather article, individually, to complete the exercise.

When training, you have kept the articles only about six feet away from you. You will eventually want the articles placed about 15 feet from you and about six inches apart. As you are working with the dog, if you find that he is continuously bringing the wrong article, try placing the articles further apart and also try scenting them more thoroughly.

Some of you may experience hesitancy on the part of the dog to leave your side and go after the article. If this happens, walk part of the way with your dog, thus reassuring him that this is what you want him to do. When he reaches the articles, back up slowly to your original position.

Don't forget that praise! Be quick to give it. Remember

Once the dog is working proficiently, the handler must remain silent and motionless as the dog returns with the article.

The dog must sit directly in front of the handler holding the article until the out *command is given.*

your dog is constantly trying to please you. If you forget to praise him, how is he going to know what you really want? You must apply the same reference to your commands. They should be definite. This does not mean boisterous or menacing. They can be moderately toned and given calmly and yet still be demanding. The dog must be able to distinguish between praise and command. These two factors, along with repetition, are necessary to his learning process.

I am sure by this time that you realize this exercise cannot be accomplished without considerable effort on your part. The actual function of smelling is a natural instinct of the dog. Although some dogs have a keener sense of smell than others, it will have no bearing on how he performs this exercise. All dogs with a sense of smell can learn this exercise equally well. You have the responsibility of developing this natural instinct to a useful and pleasurable purpose.

Some of you who are training your dogs for practical purposes and not for competition in AKC trials may feel that this exercise is too complicated and time consuming for everyday use. Quickly put aside this misconception. It is one of the most practical of all the obedience exercises. Just think how nice it would be someday when you drop a personal possession, such as your key ring in the backyard and instead of crawling around on your knees to look for it, you simply give your dog the scent and tell him to *get it*!

17
The Send-Out

THE SEND-OUT CAN BE USED FOR PRACTICAL PURPOSES OR IN preparation for showing your dog in American Kennel Club Trials in conjunction with the bar and solid jumps.

Begin this exercise with the lead on the dog and have him sitting in the correct heel position. Holding the lead with your right hand only, use your left hand to make a sweeping forward motion simultaneously commanding the dog *run*. Immediately upon giving these commands, start running with your dog. As you are progressing forward, try to fall back a few steps behind the dog. Continue giving the command *run* as the dog goes ahead. Do not fall back any further than the length of the lead will allow.

If you are using the recommended six-foot lead, permit the dog to go about five feet ahead of you. This will give you an excess of one foot. As soon as the dog will move ahead this distance then call his name, follow up instantly with the command *sit*. When you call the dog's name, you are attempting to get the dog to turn toward you, so that when the *sit* command is given, the dog will automatically sit facing you. If the dog responds, be sure to praise him. If he does not sit, simply step into him, and, with your left hand, jerk smartly upward on the lead, forcing him to sit. At this point, praise him. This will indicate to him, even if you had to help, that this is what you want.

You will then walk to the dog. Do not call him. Repeat this exercise on lead until your dog is willing to leave your side without hesitation. Be sure to use the hand signal and the command *run* as often as necessary. When you feel that you have successfully conquered this portion of the exercise, then you may begin off lead.

Once again, with the dog in the proper heel position, give the hand signal and the verbal command *run*. Take a few steps with the dog gradually falling back. Encourage him

With the dog in the proper heel position, give the hand signal and the verbal command to run.

Your ultimate goal is to get the dog to run without you to a distance of about 40 feet.

to progress forward without you, if he seems confused, then run with him. Be careful that you do not inadvertently give any heel commands or you will defeat your purpose.

Your ultimate goal is to get the dog to run without you to a distance of about 40 feet. When the dog is completely trained, you will be permitted to give the hand signal along with the verbal command *run*, but only once. When he has reached the desired distance, then you are permitted to call his name, followed immediately with the command *sit*.

While working with the dog off lead, if he seems consistently reluctant to go any distance on command, try placing something such as an opened handkerchief on the ground at the proper distance to entice him. As soon as he reaches the handkerchief, be ready to call his name and give the sit command. You should try to prevent him from picking up the object, by being quick to give the commands.

Some dogs will develop the habit of turning several times while running out. Try to prevent this by quickly repeating the run command the instant the dog seems to hesitate. Soon, he will realize that he must continue for a rather lengthly distance and this will help to prevent turning.

You must never allow the dog to turn at his own discretion. If he turns on his own, without hesitation give the *run* command. Always be sure that your commands are distinct. Remember that the dog is hearing these commands from a distance. This is especially true of the sit command. In some instances, the dog will either stand or lie down when he turns. Do not be too disturbed with this. Simply walk out to him and force him to sit. Follow immediately with praise. He will soon get the idea.

This exercise must be progressed gradually. You cannot expect the dog to run 30 or 40 feet until he has learned specifically what is expected of him. On the other hand, you will find that this exercise, if methodically practiced, will be accomplished with relative ease.

18
Directed Jumping

THE DIFFERENCE BETWEEN DIRECTED JUMPING AND THE PREVIously learned jumping exercises is that you will use both the bar jump and the solid jump, and you will designate by direction which jump you want the dog to take.

Before you can begin this exercise, you should have the send-out perfected. If you have accomplished this, then take both the solid jump and the bar jump and place them about 20 feet apart, opposite one another.

When setting up the jumps for this exercise, remember the specifications given previously for your particular breed of dog. It is advisable in the beginning however, to keep the jumps somewhat lower than the maximum height required for your dog. This will make it easier for him to clear the jump, because your main concern will be to get him to take direction.

Stand with your dog in the heel position, facing the jumps about 20 feet away from them. Start by practicing the send-out between the two jumps. Your objective at this point is to get the dog to run between the jumps, and respond to your sit command correctly.

DIRECTED JUMPING/161

Remember when practicing this portion of the exercise that when the dog sits on your command, never call him to you. You walk out to him and heel him back to the original position at your side facing the jumps. The reason for this is evident: If you encouraged the dog to come to you between the jumps, he would naturally assume that it is all right to avoid them. You would have created a problem that you would just have to correct later on.

You must insist that the dog go a distance of about 20 feet beyond the two jumps and as nearly as possible in a straight line. If the dog persists in going slightly to the left or right of the center, you may permit this. However, you cannot allow him to veer too much in either direction.

The dog should be sitting about 20 feet beyond the two jumps—as nearly as possible an equal distance between them.

Once you have obtained a good send-out, then you may begin the actual directed jumping. It is advisable to move into a position only about 10 feet away from the jumps until the dog gets accustomed to taking direction. Determining which jump should be on the left and which one should be to the right is at your own discretion. This makes no difference and will have no bearing on the dog's performance. The dog will undoubtedly favor the jump that he is most familiar with in the beginning, but this is only a natural reaction and will be overcome with practice.

For the first few sessions, commence by using the jump to your right. Give your dog the hand signal and command to *run*. As soon as he is the appropriate distance away from the jumps, call his name and give the command *sit*. Then with your right arm and hand extended directly from the shoulder parallel with the jump, command *jump*. You may preface the command with the dog's name. However, you must follow immediately with the signal and verbal command to *jump*.

If your dog seems reluctant, then run up to the designated jump and tap it on the top, repeating the command *jump*. As soon as the dog responds, back up immediately to your original position. Be sure that you do not block his way when he starts to jump. You are permitted to alter your position so that you are facing the direction in which the dog is returning. However, you cannot turn toward him until he is in mid-air over the jump.

When teaching the dog this particular exercise, your commands should be kept clear and audible at all times. They should be given in a rather spirited tone. Your timing is again of the utmost importance. You must be very careful that your signals and verbal commands are given at exactly the right moment. This will have a great deal of influence on your success with this exercise.

When you feel that you are progressing successfully, then you may undertake the final stages of the exercise. Still keeping the jumps at a height that is somewhat lower than required for your dog, start by standing approximately 20 feet behind the jumps. Be sure that you are in a position that is an equal distance between the two jumps.

With the dog sitting in the proper heel position, verbally command and simultaneously give the hand signal for the dog to run. Your dog should run briskly and in a reasonably straight line to an area about 20 feet beyond the jumps. Remember, the dog should not turn until you call his name and give the command to *sit*.

Then, extending your left arm and hand in a parallel position with the jump on the left, give the jump command. You must give the verbal command to *jump* the instant your arm completes the point. As soon as the dog is in the air over the jump, you may pivot a 45 degree angle to await your dog to come and sit in front of you. Complete the exercise with the usual *heel* command.

Once the dog takes the left direction equally as well as the right, then you can begin to alternate directions. At a point and time when you feel the dog is performing the exercises with confidence, raise the jumps to the required height for your breed.

Let's discuss some of the problems that you may encounter with this exercise and their possible solutions. One that is fairly common is that the dog will become confused and attempt to take the jump on the way out. This can be resolved by moving into a position between the jumps for the send-out. He cannot possibly take the jumps from this position. After you have given the sit command, back up several feet and give the direction. Practice this procedure until he gets the idea that he is to jump only when commanded.

You may also find that the dog will respond to the jump

The Left-Directed Jump

The Right-Directed Jump

command, but repeatedly ignores your direction and takes the jump that catches his eye. The basic problem here is inattention. It is not that he doesn't understand your signal, he simply is not looking and concentrating on what you are doing. There are several possible solutions for this problem depending upon your individual needs. Since you are permitted to use the dog's name just prior to the jump command, do so. This can get the attention of a dog that is looking around. You may also take into consideration your hand signal. Are you holding it too long? Not only are you not permitted to hold a signal when competing in AKC trials, you could be giving the dog too much time to catch your signal. This creates an atmosphere in which he feels he has all the time he wants to get the signal, so he simply doesn't pay attention.

Now for some discussion on what to do if the dog does start to take the wrong jump. *Do not permit it.* The command *no* should be given emphatically, thereby stopping him immediately. The next step is to start the exercise all over. Bring him back to the heel position and do the send-out over again. Since your dog is already familiar with *no*, he will realize instantly that something is wrong. By repeating this phase of the exercise in its entirety you are conveying to him the correct procedure. Keep practicing this until he takes the originally designated jump.

When you and your dog are completing this exercise with a reasonable amount of reliability, each day as you begin your practice session set the jumps in an alternate position from the way they were the day before. You do not want the bar jump, for example, on the same side every day. Another point to remember when practicing: Do not always give the same direction first each day. Keeping an awareness of these two simple procedures will avoid establishing an undesirable pattern.

19
The Directed Retrieve

FOR THIS EXERCISE, YOU WILL AGAIN ADD SOME EQUIPMENT TO your collection. It will consist of three predominantly white gloves. It is necessary to use white gloves so that your dog can easily see them.

Begin with your dog sitting in the heel position, off lead. For practice, throw one of the gloves, as if it were the dumbbell, in a straight line ahead of you. Command the dog to *take*. Repeat this basic retrieve several times to get the dog used to handling the glove.

With your dog sitting in the proper heel position, command the dog to *stay*. Walk straight ahead for approximately 20 feet, and place the glove on the ground. Then return to your dog. Stoop to a position equal to your dog's eye level. Extend your left arm in a straight line and with a distinct motion point directly to the glove; command the dog to *take*. If your dog shows signs of hesitation, then take a couple of steps with him for encouragement. If necessary, the first few times go to the glove with him. The moment that the dog picks up the glove, back up a few steps thereby allowing him to carry the glove to you until you have reached the original starting point. Be sure to praise your dog enthusiastically for taking the glove. When you are both in position, take the glove from his mouth using the command *out*. Then command him to *heel*, and he will be back in the proper heel position.

The next step is to place another glove in a straight line 15 feet to the left of the original center glove. Now you have two gloves for the dog to work with. One is directly straight ahead and the other is to the left.

You will always start this exercise from the same position, that is, facing straight ahead in the direction of the center glove. But to get into position for the left glove, obviously you must turn. This is accomplished by pivoting briskly to your left and commanding the dog to *heel*. Repeat the above described procedure for giving direction with one exception—that by giving the arm direction properly in the line of vision, you can advantageously block the dog's vision of the center glove.

Now for the placement of the third and final glove. It should be located in a straight line 15 feet to the right of the center glove. At this point, you should have three gloves encompassing a total of 30 feet in width, all in a straight line, a distance of about 20 feet away from you.

Once again, facing straight ahead, command the dog to heel and pivot to the right. Stoop to the proper position, and give the signal and the command to *take* in the direction of the right glove.

You will probably find that the right glove is the most difficult for the average dog, because you cannot block his view from the remaining two gloves. Until he becomes proficient in performing this entire exercise, you will undoubtedly have a problem with the dog going to the incorrect glove. If this happens to you, do not allow the dog to actually pick up the wrong glove. Simply give the command *no* and call the dog back to you. Then repeat the exercise, using the same glove, until he takes your direction correctly.

If you find that you are consistently experiencing problems with end gloves, be sure that when you pivot toward the left or right glove the dog is in the proper heel position. That will automatically put him in line with the correct glove.

The purpose of this exercise is not to teach the dog to retrieve but to retrieve a designated object. Undoubtedly, you will feel a great sense of pride when you can point to any object several feet away from you and end up with it in your hand.

To give the signal, stoop to a position equal to your dog's eye level.

If the dog shows confidence, allow him to progress to the designated glove alone.

While training, be quick to give him plenty of verbal praise when he returns with the glove.

Use the standard out *command as you remove the glove from the dog's mouth.*

20
Yard-Breaking Your Dog

THERE IS ONE INEVITABLE QUESTION THAT ALWAYS ARISES WITH dog owners. "How can I guarantee that my dog will stay in the yard? My answer is, "Fence your yard."

This statement is made with the full realization that it will bring immediate controversial response from those persons who firmly believe that their dog will not stray. To further emphasize my opinion, permit me to ask the question, Would you stake your dog's life on the fact that he is completely dependable, under any circumstance? Because, unfortunately, that is what you are doing.

However, this does not mean that the situation cannot be controlled. It can be handled quite effectively with the proper training and reasonable supervision. By teaching your dog his hypothetical boundary lines, you can enjoy play periods with your dog off lead in the yard and also allow him to be free to perform his chores while supervising from a reasonable distance.

To properly train a dog to remain in his yard while being supervised, begin by taking your dog out on a 30-foot line. You can purchase training leads of this length, but if you do not wish to buy one, simply make one of clothes line. Allow him freedom to the extent of walking to the very edge of your property. Be sure to allow slack in the line at all times. At the exact moment he starts to take a step off your property, command sharply *no*.

From the tone of your voice, most dogs will stop immediately. Then quickly, in a very pleasant tone of voice, call the dog to you. As soon as the dog reaches you, give plenty of abundant praise. However, if your dog ignores your commands, then give a quick snap of the lead, accompanied by the word *come*. Follow with immediate physical praise.

Once the dog begins to realize his boundaries and will respond faultlessly to your commands of *no* and *come*, then you many take him off lead. It is advisable, in the beginning, to decrease the distance between you and the dog until you are sure that you have the verbal control necessary to keep him within his limitations. If he reacts favorably, then you may gradually increase the distance until you reach the amount of space you desire. You must use good judgment in this respect. Any reasonably sized property will not present a problem. However, if you have large acreage, then you must establish your own boundaries for the dog.

The main obstacle that presents itself with this particular training is that the trainer might become overanxious. You must perform this phase of training with the same patience and the same routine as you would any form of obedience work. You can have two or three practice sessions daily of about 10 to 15 minutes. During the period of time while the dog is being taught yard-breaking, you cannot permit intervals when the rules do not apply. You must be consistent.

Another basic rule that must be firmly adhered to when yard-breaking your dog is that you must never indicate any form of displeasure with your dog once you have given the command to come. The dog must always be able to associate pleasure with the act of coming to you when called. If you experience any difficulty in getting him to respond to you, then kneel down and clap your hands. This usually creates a favorable reaction from the dog.

Teaching your dog to remain in his yard, off lead, is the sincere desire of almost everyone who owns a dog. Once the training has been accomplished, the key to continued success is supervision. Under normal circumstances, your dog can be taught to be very dependable. But we must allow for those few times when some compelling curiosity presents itself across the street or next door. It is not logical to expect, even the most well-trained dog, to remain in the yard, unattended, for indefinite periods of time. But, in exchange for a few hours of your time and a little patience, you will be able to enjoy your dog's companionship during those family gatherings in the backyard during the summer months.

21
The Dog and the Family Automobile

THERE ARE MANY OCCASIONS WHEN ALL OF YOU FIND IT necessary or desirable to take your dogs with you in the family automobile. You will not find a more serviceable use for much of your obedience training than in this particular instance.

Although most dogs find riding in the car a most pleasurable undertaking, many of them can be difficult to get in and out of the car. To begin, take the dog on lead to the car. Tell him to sit and give the command *stay*, then open the car door. To prevent the overanxious dog from entering the car of his own volition, enforce the stay command. Then follow up with the *jump* command. Immediately follow with the sit or down command, whichever you prefer for riding purposes. Simply reverse the procedure for an orderly departure from the automobile.

What about the dog that likes to ride, but is reluctant to get in or out of the car by himself? This too, can be remedied with patience and proper training. You will use the same basic procedure as stated previously. If your dog is sufficiently familiar with the sit, stay, and jump commands, you will be pleased to find how quickly he will trust your judgment and obey your commands. The prime requisite here is patience. Do not attempt to alter such a situation when you are in a hurry. More often than not, this procedure will have to be practiced several times, the same as any obedience lesson, to obtain perfection. Be alert when closing the car doors that the dog is completely out of the way and behaving as he should. This will prevent any possibility of getting tails and feet caught in the doors.

For safety reasons, the dog's lead should be removed while riding in the car. This will prevent him from becoming entangled in the lead and possibly getting hurt. It will be to your advantage to insist that the dog always ride in he back seat. This will prevent the dog from being tossed against the dashboard or the windshield in case of a sudden stop. However, unlikely as it may seem, there is always the possibility that even the most well-trained dog will become excited over something he sees and suddenly lunge into your lap while you are driving if he is allowed to sit in the front seat.

Another common problem is car sickness. This can be helped and usually cured by taking the dog for several very short rides over a period of time. Naturally, it is recommended that you do not give this type any dog food or water before taking him in the car. If after a reasonable time, your dog cannot adjust to riding in the automobile without getting sick, then consult your vet for further advice or perhaps medication.

Although proper ventilation, even while riding, is an absolute must for your dog, do not allow him to project his body from the automobile in any way while riding. You have probably seen cars traveling down the highway with a dog's head or even half of his body protruding from the moving vehicle. Common sense tells us that it would take very little for that dog to be thrown completely out of the car. Not only is the overall situation dangerous, but the wind blowing into the dog's face so forcefully can be injurious to his eyes.

Probably the most innocently abused rule of all is leaving your dog unattended in your automobile. In my opinion, this is a positive *no*. First of all, you cannot safely provide sufficient oxygen for your dog to breathe. Next, even the most docile dog will sometimes become very protective of the car. This can create problems with curious strangers. Then there is the dog that becomes extremely frightened at being left alone and will destroy the interior of your car trying to get out. I, personally, can think of no logical reason why your dog should be left by himself in the car for an extended time. Therefore, when you can't stay with your dog in the car, rather than be met by some unforseen tragedy, wouldn't it be better to be met by a wagging tail at home?

22
Cold Weather Care of the Dog

LET'S CONSIDER SOME PROS AND CONS PERTAINING TO PROPER care of the dog during cold weather.

For those of you who have a dog that is kept outdoors all the time, one of the most important items for you to take in to account is clean and comfortable quarters. You should provide a doghouse that is free of drafts and has only a large enough opening to accomodate your particular breed. The floor of the doghouse should be made of wood and situated at least four inches above the ground level. His bedding can consist of cedar shavings, straw, or shredded newspapers. These materials are preferred because they do not retain dampness and the dog can manipulate these loose materials to his liking. When constructing your dog's home, keep the cold weather in mind and try to situate it so that the doorway will not face into the wind. The area around the doghouse should be checked to make sure that there are no ruts or low spots so as to provide as dry an area as possible for your pet.

Keep your outdoor dog supplied with plenty of fresh water. Frequent checking is necessary as his water will freeze surprisingly fast. It is advisable to provide his water in an unbreakable container. It is my opinion that late feeding is preferrable during the winter season. Your dog's body will become more active during the process of digestion and will provide heat during the night while he sleeps if you feed him rather late in the evening. Be sure that, without overfeeding, your dog gets plenty to eat.

Proper care of your dog's coat and nails are also prime requisites for suitable winter care of your dog. The nails should be kept short to prevent the snow from packing into them and causing extreme discomfort. Daily brushing is a necessity. This will not only stimulate the growth of a thick, warm undercoat, but gives you the opportunity to keep a continuous check on his coat condition. A dog's skin can become dry and flaky from the cold weather just as ours would. A little cod liver oil or any coat conditioner added to the daily diet can help alleviate the dry skin and enhance the beauty of his coat.

The dog that is kept indoors requires the same good grooming as the outdoor dog. His nails and coat must be given just as much attention as he will be going out into the snow and cold periodically. The owner of an indoor dog must be aware of the length of time that his dog remains outside in the winter. Of course, your dog does have a certain amount of natural resistance to cold weather, but because he has the advantage of being kept in a well-heated home, his coat adjusts accordingly and therefore may leave him somewhat unprepared for extended sessions outdoors.

Now for the subject of the indoor-outdoor dog. This is a perfectly acceptable combination for the summer months and warm climates. I, personally, do not recommend this for the winter months. It seems reasonable that the dog's body will not adjust instantaneously to drastic changes in temperatures. Therefore, it would be a good idea to make a decision during the late summer as to the winter accommodations for your dog and abide by them.

23
Warm Weather Care of the Dog

THE WARM, SUNNY DAYS OF THE SUMMER ARE WELCOMED BY canine members of our society with the same enthusiasm that we hold for pleasant outdoor weather. There are, however, some important considerations that should be taken into account pertaining to the proper care of our dogs during the hot weather.

First on the agenda, for the outdoor dog, is that the same proper housing be provided as required for the winter months—dry and partially shaded. Additional bedding is not a necessity during the warm months, but can be used if your dog seems to prefer it. Keep in mind that if extra bedding is used, it should be changed more frequently than during the winter. The doghouse, itself, should be sterilized regularly. If your dog is provided with a cement run, then this too, should be disinfected.

Your dog must, as in the winter, be well supplied with fresh, clean water. This not only will keep him more comfortable but will prevent an overindulgence of water at a given time, due to excessive thirst. Continue your late feeding schedule during hot weather, but for a different reason. His body will not have to perform digestive functions during the extreme heat of the day.

Caring for your dog's coat during hot weather need not present a problem. Daily brushing will be the biggest factor in keeping his coat in proper condition. It not only keeps him comfortable and helps prevent skin diseases, but it will eliminate the need for "excessive" bathing. For those of you who own breeds with heavy undercoats, there is an additional precaution that must be taken pertaining to bathing. The weather should be ideal, that is, warm but not humid. The dog should be artificially dried as much as possible and he should be bathed early enough in the day so as to be completely dry by the time he retires for the night. There are also many dry shampoos that can be used quite effectively to cleanse the dog's coat.

Exertion and exposure to heat are other factors that must be controlled during the summer. Winter activity, age, overall health, and the breed of your dog will determine just how much exercise and exposure he can physically accommodate. No dog should be permitted to romp around until a reasonable time has elapsed after each feeding. You must be especially careful with the large, heavy breeds. Another important factor to be considered is air conditioning. The dog's body will adjust to those conditions to which he is exposed the majority of the time. Therefore, when he is subjected to extreme changes in temperature, good judgment must be employed by you in relation to the amount of exercise and the length of time involved.

When vacation time rolls around, whether you decide to take the dog along or board him with a reputable individual, you should make certain provisions for his care. Whenever possible, make available to him an adequate supply of the water he is normally accustomed to drinking.

If it is at all feasible, try to maintain the same diet and if he is left with someone, give them the name and location of the veterinarian you wish to be called in case of an emergency. If you so desire, you may leave with him some items belonging to the family with which he can associate. If your decision is to take the dog with you, then try to make reservations in advance for lodging that will accommodate your dog.

Properly caring for one's dog is a responsibility. However, by performing a few simple daily functions and remembering to include the welfare of the dog in your family plans, you can, with very little effort, provide him with a good home.

24
Attack Training vs Watchdog

A COMMON QUESTION THAT CONSTANTLY PRESENTS ITSELF TO anyone associated with dog training is, "How can I attack-train my dog"? My answer is always the same. Leave the attack training of dogs to the professional.

As for having a reliable watchdog, almost every dog has that quality already built-in. All dogs possess a natural instinct to protect what they understand to be theirs. This unconscious skill can be exaggerated or diminished by environmental influences.

Most house dogs will respond to the ringing of a doorbell or a knock on the door by barking profusely. A kennel dog will alert you the moment someone approaches your property by profound barking. This does not necessarily mean that they will bite, but is usually sufficient to ward off an unwanted intruder.

Attack training a dog requires a great deal of skill and experience. This particular phase of dog training should never be attempted by amateurs. All too often, unsuspecting dog owners are victims of the many fallacies relative to creating a good guard dog. Don't allow yourself to become involved in creating a situation that will bring only unhappiness to you and your dog.

Many dogs having received expert training in the field of guard or attack work are used quite effectively by department stores and law enforcement agencies. These dogs are, however, handled by individuals who are equally well trained and respect their potential.

The average homeowner's needs can be met by the dog of his choice, regardless of size. Basically what we all want is for our dog to alert us to the presence of strangers. A small dog can make just as much noise as a large one.

In order to encourage your dog to perform as a watchdog, always react favorably when he draws your attention to any movement or noises that disturb him. This can be done quite simply by going with him to investigate the source. Even if there is nothing visible or audible to you, trust his keen senses and praise him for calling your attention to the problem.

This does not mean, however, that you must allow your dog to bark incessantly at his own discretion. After checking the reason for his barking, you determine that the situation does not warrant any concern, the dog can be commanded firmly *no*. He will soon learn that you are more than willing to pay attention to his warning, but it is not necessary for him to continue barking once you have checked out the matter.

You may find yourself spending quite a bit of time checking all the neighborhood cats and rabbits bounding across your yard, but you must be tolerant of your dog's persistence if you expect him to perform when it is necessary.

If there is still an individual who feels that for some professional or personal reason, he needs a guard dog, then by all means consult a qualified expert in the field of guard dog training.

25
The Shy Dog

THE SHY DOG IS QUITE COMMON AND IS ONE THAT REQUIRES considerable attention. Tendencies toward shynesss are usually apparent quite early in puppyhood.

Let's discuss first, how you can recognize shyness. A shy dog will find comfort in hiding behind the handler and in many cases will growl and even snap at anyone who approaches them. Some dogs will seek a remote corner of a particular room as a hideaway. Others will become overly possessive of a particular individual in the family and use this person as a means of protection.

One of the first things the owner of this type of dog should do is get the dog out in public as soon as possible. Take him (on lead) for walks in your neighborhood and encourage him to investigate curiosities he seems to be wary of. If he tries to hide behind you, by all means use the lead to guide him to your side. All the while using a soothing tone of voice to give encouragement to the dog.

The next step should be basic obedience training with particular emphasis on the stand for examination. Keep in mind that a shy dog will need some added patience and understanding on your part to successfully accomplish this exercise. Stand your dog in the normal manner, but remain at his side in the heel position. Then, using your left hand apply some pressure to different areas of the dog's back and hindquarters. Please do not press too hard, just enough so that the dog will resist your press. The idea is to relate to the dog that he must remain standing under any circumstance.

Once you have the dog standing with a reasonable amount of confidence, then have a second party approach him. This individual should approach the dog without hesitation and proceed to touch the dog from his head, down the back of the neck, and over the entire length of his body. If he resists, then you must restrain him and repeat the experience until you are successful. Continue with this until you are able to leave the dog approximately six feet and he will remain standing for any individual to inspect him.

When friends visit you, it would be most helpful if they would assist you with your problem by sitting calmly in a particular chair and just speaking to your dog in a pleasant tone. Allow the dog to warm up to strangers at his own speed. With your permission, they might try gaining his friendship with a biscuit or some other tidbit that meets with your approval. You should be cautious that strangers in your home do not make any sudden unexpected movements as this is a startling experience for the shy dog and will undoubtedly be greeted with disapproval by him.

Of course, one of the most common questions concerning shy dogs is—will they bite? It is my opinion that under a given circumstance, they will. You must understand that for them this will occur only as a last resort. The shy dog has no ill intent other than to ward off what he believes to be dangerous to himself or his loved ones. It is also my contention that a truly shy dog can never completely overcome his shyness, but can be taught to tolerate sharing his world with other living creatures, both human and animal.

It is also my firm belief that it is more important for the

shy dog to understand without question, the difference beween right and wrong than it is for the so-called normal-tempered dog. This means that you must assume a great deal of responsibility to this animal. You will find that this type of dog will stabilize much more readily when he realizes without question what you expect of him. He must know that your commands are not to be ignored, but that you, without a doubt, are trustworthy.

There is no short cut in learning to handle the shy dog. It takes much time and infinite patience. Your primary concern will be to instill confidence in your dog. Do not take this lightly. The shy dog experiences fear beyond your comprehension. Do not interpret his reluctance to obey at times as obstinacy; it is simply apprehension. Keep the lines of communication open at all times.

The author and Caesar take a few moments from their training to just enjoy each other's company.

188/DOG OBEDIENCE TRAINING

Dorian Gray joins the author for that all important "play period" after a training session.

Appendix

Obedience Regulations of the American Kennel Club

Purpose

Obedience trials are a sport and all participants should be guided by the principles of good sportsmanship both in and outside of the ring. The purpose of obedience trials is to demonstrate the usefulness of the pure-bred dog as a companion of man, not merely the dog's ability to follow specified routines in the obedience ring. While all contestants in a class are required to perform the same exercises in substantially the same way so that the relative quality of the various performances may be compared and scored, the basic objective of obedience trials is to produce dogs that have been trained and conditioned always to behave in the home, in public places, and in the presence of other dogs, in a manner that will reflect credit on the sport of obedience. The performances of dog and handler in the ring must be accurate and correct and must conform to the requirements of these regulations. However, it is also essential that the dog demonstrate willingness and enjoyment of its work, and smoothness and naturalness on the part of the handler are to be preferred to a performance based on military precision and peremptory commands.

CHAPTER 1
General Regulations

Section 1. **Obedience Clubs.** An obedience club that meets all the requirements of The American Kennel Club and wishes to hold an Obedience Trial at which qualifying scores toward an obedience title may be awarded, must make application to The American Kennel Club on the form provided for permission to hold such trial. Such a trial, if approved, may be held either in conjunction with a dog show or as a separate event. If the club is not a member of The American Kennel Club it shall pay a license fee for the privilege of holding such trial, the amount of which shall be determined by the Board of Directors of The American Kennel Club. If the club fails to hold its trial at the time and place which have been approved, the amount of the license fee paid will be returned.

Section 2. **Dog Show and Specialty Clubs.** A dog show club may be granted permission to hold a licensed or member obedience trial at its dog show, and a specialty club may also be granted permission to hold a licensed or member obedience trial if, in the opinion of the Board of Directors of The American Kennel Club, such clubs are qualified to do so.

Section 3. **Obedience Classes.** A licensed or member obedience trial need not include all of the regular obedience classes defined in this chapter, but a club will be approved to hold Open classes only if it also holds Novice classes, and a club will be approved to hold a Utility class only if it also holds Novice and Open classes. A specialty club which has been approved to hold a licensed or member obedience trial, if qualified in the opinion of the Board of Directors of The American Kennel Club, or an obedience club which has been approved to hold a licensed or member obedience trial may, subject to the approval of The American Kennel Club, offer additional non-regular classes for dogs not less than six months of age, provided a clear and complete description of the eligibility requirements and performance requirements for each such class appears in the premium list. Pre-Novice classes will not be approved at licensed or member obedience trials.

Section 4. **Tracking Tests.** A club that has been approved to hold licensed or member obedience trials and that meets the requirements of The American Kennel Club, may also make application to hold a Tracking Test. A club may not hold a tracking test on the same day as its show or obedience trial, but the tracking test may be announced in the premium list for the show or trial, and the tracking test entries may be included in the show or obedience trial catalog. If the entries are not listed in the catalog for the show or obedience trial, the club must provide, at the tracking test, several copies of a sheet, which may be typewritten, giving all the information that would be contained in the catalog for each entered dog. If the tracking test is to be held within 7 days of the obedience trial the entries must be sent to the same person designated to receive the obedience trial entries, and the same closing date should apply. If the tracking test is not to be held within 7 days of the obedience trial the club may name someone else in the premium list to receive the tracking test entries, and may specify a different closing date for entries at least 7 days before the tracking test.

The presence of a veterinarian shall not be required at a tracking test.

Section 5. **Obedience Trial Committee.** If an obedience trial is held by an obedience club, an Obedience Trial Committee must be appointed by the club, and this committee shall exercise all the authority vested in a dog show's Bench Show Committee. If an obedience club holds its obedience trial in conjunction with a dog show, then the Obedience Trial Committee shall have sole jurisdiction only over those dogs entered in the obedience trial and their handlers and owners; provided, however, that if any dog is entered in both obedience and breed classes, then the Obedience Trial Committee shall have jurisdiction over such dog, its owner, and its handler, only in matters pertaining to the Obedience Regulations, and the Bench Show Committee shall have jurisdiction over such dog, its owner and handler, in all other matters.

When an obedience trial is to be held in conjunction with a dog show by the club which has been granted permission to hold the show, the club's Bench Show Committee shall include one person designated as "Obedience Chairman". At such event the Bench Show Committee of the show-giving club shall have sole jurisdiction over all matters which may properly come before it, regardless of whether the matter has to do with the dog show or with the obedience trial.

Section 6. **Sanctioned Matches.** A club may hold an Obedience Match by obtaining the sanction of The American Kennel Club. Sanctioned obedience matches shall be governed by such regulations as may be adopted by the Board of Directors of The American Kennel Club. Scores awarded at such matches will not be entered in the records of The American Kennel Club nor count towards an obedience title.

All of these Obedience Regulations shall also apply to sanctioned matches except for those sections in which it is specified that the provisions apply to licensed or member trials, and except where specifically stated otherwise in the Regulations for Sanctioned Matches.

Section 7. **American Kennel Club Sanction.** American Kennel Club sanction must be obtained by any club that holds American Kennel Club obedience trials, for any type of match for which it solicits or accepts entries from non-members.

Section 8. **Dog Show Rules.** All the Dog Show Rules, where applicable, shall govern the conducting of obedience trials and tracking tests, and shall apply to all persons and dogs participating in them except as these Obedience Regulations may provide otherwise.

Section 9. **Immediate Family.** As used in this chapter, "immediate family" means husband, wife, father, mother, son, daughter, brother, or sister.

Section 10. **Pure-Bred Dogs Only.** As used in these regulations the word "dog" refers to either sex but only to dogs that are pure-bred of a breed eligible for registration in the American Kennel Club stud book or for entry in the Miscellaneous Class at American Kennel Club dog shows, as only such dogs may compete in obedience trials, tracking tests, or sanctioned matches. A judge must report to The American Kennel Club after the trial or tracking test any dog shown under him which in his opinion appears not to be pure-bred.

Section 11. **Unregistered Dogs.** Chapter 16, Section 1 of the Dog Show Rules shall apply to entries in licensed or member obedience trials and tracking tests, except that an eligible unregistered dog for which an ILP number has been issued by The American Kennel Club may be entered indefinitely in such events provided the ILP number is shown on each entry form.

Section 12. **Dogs That May Not Compete.** No dog belonging wholly or in part to a judge or to a Show or Obedience Trial Secretary, Superintendent, or veterinarian, or to any member of such person's immediate family or household, shall be entered in any dog show, obedience trial, or tracking test at which such person officiates or is scheduled to officiate. This applies to both obedience and dog show judges when an obedience trial is held in conjunction with a dog show. However, a tracking test shall be considered a separate event for the purpose of this section.

No dogs shall be entered or shown under a judge at an obedience trial or tracking test if the dog has been owned, sold, held under lease, handled in the ring, boarded, or has been regularly trained or instructed, within one year prior to the date of the obedience trial or tracking test, by the judge or by any member of his immediate family or household, and no such dog shall be eligible to compete. "Trained or instructed" applies equally to judges who train professionally or as amateurs, and to judges who train individual dogs or who train or instruct dogs in classes with or through their handlers.

Section 13. **When Titles Are Won.** Where any of the following sections of the regulations excludes from a particular obedience class dogs that have won a particular obedience title, eligibility to enter that class shall be determined as follows: a dog may continue to be shown in such a class after its handler has been notified by three different judges that it has received three qualifying scores for such title, but may not be entered or shown in such a class in any obedience trial of which the closing date for entries occurs after the owner has received official notification from The American Kennel Club that the dog has won the particular obedience title.

Where any of the following sections of the regulations requires that a dog shall have won a particular obedience title before competing in a particular obedience class, a dog may not be shown in such class at any obedience trial before the owner has received official notification from The American Kennel Club that the dog has won the required title.

Section 14. **Disqualification and Ineligibility.** A dog that is blind or deaf or that has been changed in appearance by artificial means (except for such changes as are customarily approved for its breed) may not compete in any obedience trial or tracking test and must be disqualified. Blind means having useful vision in neither eye. Deaf means without useful hearing.

When a judge finds any of these conditions in any dog he is judging, he shall disqualify the dog marking his book "Disqualified" and stating the reason. He shall not obtain the opinion of the show veterinarian.

The judge must disqualify any dog that attempts to attack any person in the ring. He may excuse a dog that attacks another dog or that appears dangerous to other dogs in the ring. He shall mark the dog disqualified or excused and state the reason in his judge's book, and shall give the Superintendent or Show or Trial Secretary a brief report of the dog's actions which shall be submitted to AKC with the report of the show or trial.

When a dog has been disqualified under this section as being blind or deaf or having been changed in appearance by artificial means or for having attempted to attack a person in the ring, all awards made to the dog at the trial shall be cancelled by The American Kennel Club and the dog may not again compete unless and until, following application by the owner to The American Kennel Club, the owner has received official notification from The American Kennel Club that the dog's eligibility has been reinstated.

Spayed bitches, castrated dogs, monorchid or cryptorchid males, and dogs that have faults which would disqualify them under the standards for their breeds, may compete in obedience trials if otherwise eligible under these regulations.

A dog that is lame in the ring at any obedience trial or at a tracking test may not compete and shall not receive any score at the trial. It shall be the judge's responsibility to determine whether a dog is lame. He shall not obtain the opinion of the show veterinarian. If in the judge's opinion a dog in the ring is lame, he shall not score such dog, and shall promptly excuse it from the ring and mark his book "Excused—lame".

No dog shall be eligible to compete if it appears to have been dyed or colored in any way or if the coat shows evidence of chalk or powder, or if the dog has anything attached to it whether for medical or corrective purposes, for protection, for adornment or for any other reason, except for Maltese, Poodles, Shih Tzu, and Yorkshire Terriers which may be shown with the hair over the eyes tied back as they are normally shown in the breed ring. The judge at his sole discretion, may agree to judge such a dog at a later time if the offending condition has been corrected.

An obedience judge is not required to be familiar with the breed standards nor to scrutinize each dog as in dog show judging, but shall be alert for conditions which may require disqualification or exclusion under this section.

Section 15. Disturbance—Bitches in season are not permitted to compete. The judge of an obedience trial or tracking test must remove from competition any bitch in season, any dog which its handler cannot control, any handler who interferes willfully with another competitor or his dog, and any handler who abuses his dog in the ring, and may excuse from competition any dog which he considers unfit to compete, or any bitch which appears so attractive to males as to be a disturbing element. If a dog or handler is expelled or excused by a judge, the reason shall be stated in the judge's book or in a separate report.

Section 16. Novice A Class. The Novice A class shall be for dogs not less than six months of age that have not won the title C.D. No person who has previously handled a dog that has won a C.D. title in the obedience ring at a licensed or member trial, and no person who has regularly trained such a dog, may enter or handle a dog in this class. Each dog in the class must have a separate handler, who must be its owner or a member of the owner's immediate family. The same person must handle each dog in all exercises.

Section 17. Novice B Class. The Novice B class shall be for dogs not less than six months of age that have not won the title C.D. Dogs in this class may be handled by the owner or any other person. A person may handle more than one dog in this class, but each dog must have a separate handler for the Long Sit and Long Down exercises when judged in the same group. No dog may be entered in both Novice A and Novice B classes at any one trial.

Section 18. Novice Exercises and Scores. The exercises and maximum scores in the Novice classes are:

1. Heel on Leash .... 35 points
2. Stand for Examination .... 30 points
3. Heel Free .... 45 points
4. Recall .... 30 points
5. Long Sit .... 30 points
6. Long Down .... 30 points
   Maximum Total Score ....200 points

Section 19. C.D. Title. The American Kennel Club will issue a Companion Dog certificate for each registered dog, and will permit the use of the letters "C.D." after the name of each dog that has been certified by three different judges to have received scores of more than 50% of the available points in each of the six exercises and final scores of 170 or more points in Novice classes at three licensed or member obedience trials, provided the sum total of dogs that actually competed in the regular Novice classes at each trial is not less than six.

Section 20. **Open A Class.** The Open A class shall be for dogs that have won the C.D. title but have not won the title C.D.X. Obedience judges and licensed handlers may not enter or handle dogs in this class. Each dog must be handled by its owner or by a member of his immediate family. Owners may enter more than one dog in this class but the same person who handled each dog in the first five exercises must handle the same dog in the Long Sit and Long Down exercises, except that if a person has handled more than one dog in the first five exercises he must have an additional handler, who must be the owner or a member of his immediate family, for each additional dog, when more than one dog he has handled in the first five exercises is judged in the same group for the Long Sit and Long Down.

Section 21. **Open B Class.** The Open B class will be for dogs that have won the title C.D. or C.D.X. A dog may continue to compete in this class after it has won the title U.D. Dogs in this class may be handled by the owner or any other person. Owners may enter more than one dog in this class but the same person who handled each dog in the first five exercises must handle each dog in the Long Sit and Long Down exercises, except that if a person has handled more than one dog in the first five exercises he must have an additional handler for each additional dog, when more than one dog that he has handled in the first five exercises is judged in the same group for the Long Sit and Long Down. No dog may be entered in both Open A and Open B classes at any one trial.

Section 22. **Open Exercises and Scores.** The exercises and maximum scores in the Open classes are:

1. Heel Free — 40 points
2. Drop on Recall — 30 points
3. Retrieve on Flat — 25 points
4. Retrieve over High Jump — 35 points
5. Broad Jump — 20 points
6. Long Sit — 25 points
7. Long Down — 25 points
   Maximum Total Score — 200 points

Section 23. **C.D.X. Title.** The American Kennel Club will issue a Companion Dog Excellent certificate for each registered dog, and will permit the use of the letters "C.D.X." after the name of each dog that has been certified by three different judges of obedience trials to have received scores of more than 50% of the available points in each of the seven exercises and final scores of 170 or more points in Open classes at three licensed or member obedience trials, provided the sum total of dogs that actually competed in the regular Open classes at each trial is not less than six.

APPENDIX/193

Section 24. **Utility Class.** The Utility class shall be for dogs that have won the title C.D.X. Dogs that have won the title U.D. may continue to compete in this class. Dogs in this class may be handled by the owner or any other person. Owners may enter more than one dog in this class, but each dog must have a separate handler for the Group Examination when judged in the same group.

Section 25. **Division of Utility Class.** A club may choose to divide the Utility class into Utility A and Utility B classes, provided such division is approved by The American Kennel Club and is announced in the premium list. When this is done the Utility A class shall be for dogs which have won the title C.D.X. and have not won the title U.D. Obedience judges and licensed handlers may not enter or handle dogs in this class. A dog may be handled in the Group Examination by a person other than the person who handled it in the individual exercises, but each dog must be handled in all exercises by the owner or by a member of his immediate family. All other dogs that are eligible for the Utility class but not eligible for the Utility A class may be entered only in the Utility B class to which the conditions listed in Section 24 shall apply. No dog may be entered in both Utility A and Utility B classes at any one trial.

Section 26. **Utility Exercises and Scores.** The exercises and maximum scores in the Utility classes are:

1. Scent Discrimination—
   Article No. 1 — 30 points
2. Scent Discrimination—
   Article No. 2 — 30 points
3. Directed Retrieve — 30 points
4. Signal Exercise — 35 points
5. Directed Jumping — 40 points
6. Group Examination — 35 points
   Maximum Total Score — 200 points

Section 27. **U.D. Title.** The American Kennel Club will issue a Utility Dog certificate for each registered dog, and will permit the use of the letters "U.D." after the name of each dog that has been certified by three different judges of obedience trials to have received scores of more than 50% of the available points in each of the six exercises and final scores of 170 or more points in Utility classes at three licensed or member obedience trials in each of which three or more dogs actually competed in the Utility class or classes.

Section 28. **Tracking Test.** This test shall be for dogs not less than six months of age, and must be judged by two judges. With each entry form for a licensed or member tracking test for a dog that has not passed an AKC tracking test there must be filed an original written statement, dated within six months of the date the entry is received, signed by a person who has been approved by The American Kennel Club to judge tracking tests, certifying that the dog is considered by him to be ready for such a test. These original statements cannot be used again and must be submitted to The American Kennel Club with the entry forms. Written permission to waive or modify this requirement may be granted by The American Kennel Club in unusual circumstances. Tracking tests are open to all dogs that are otherwise eligible under these Regulations.

This test cannot be given at a dog show or obedience trial. The duration of this test may be one day or more within a 15 day period after the original date in the event of an unusually large entry or other unforeseen emergency, provided that the change of date is satisfactory to the exhibitors affected.

Section 29. **T.D. Title.** The American Kennel Club will issue a Tracking Dog certificate to a registered dog, and will permit the use of the letters "T.D." after the name of each dog which has been certified by the two judges to have passed a licensed or member tracking test in which at least three dogs actually participated.

The owner of a dog holding both the U.D. and T.D. titles may use the letters "U.D.T." after the name of the dog, signifying "Utility Dog Tracker".

Section 30. **Obedience Ribbons.** At licensed or member obedience trials the following colors shall be used for prize ribbons or rosettes in all regular classes:

First Prize	Blue
Second Prize	Red
Third Prize	Yellow
Fourth Prize	White
Special Prize	Dark Green

and the following colors shall be used for non-regular classes:

First Prize	Rose
Second Prize	Brown
Third Prize	Light Green
Fourth Prize	Gray

Each ribbon or rosette shall be at least two inches wide and approximately eight inches long, and shall bear on its face a facsimile of the seal of The American Kennel Club, the words "Obedience Trial", the name of the prize, the name of the trial-giving club, the date of the trial, and the name of the city or town where the trial is given.

Section 31. **Match Ribbons.** If ribbons are given at sanctioned obedience matches they shall be of the following colors and shall have the words "Obedience Match" printed on them, but may be of any design or size:

First Prize	Rose
Second Prize	Brown
Third Prize	Light Green
Fourth Prize	Gray
Special Prize	Green with pink edges

Section 32. **Prizes.** Ribbons for the four official placings and all other prizes offered for competition within a single regular class at a licensed or member trial, shall be awarded only to dogs that earn scores of more than 50% of the available points in each exercise and final scores of 170 or more points.

Prizes for which dogs in one class compete against dogs in one or more other classes at a licensed or member trial may, at the option of the club holding the trial, specify that scores of more than 50% of the available points in each exercise and final scores of 170 or more points, are required.

Ribbons and all prizes offered at sanctioned obedience matches, and in non-regular classes at licensed and member trials, shall be awarded on the basis of final scores without regard to more than 50% of the points in each exercise.

Prizes at a licensed or member obedience trial must be offered to be won outright, with the exception that a prize which requires three wins by the same owner, not necessarily with the same dog, for permanent possession, may be offered for the dog with the highest qualifying score in one of the regular classes, for the highest scoring dog in the regular classes, or for the highest combined score in the Open B and Utility classes.

Subject to the provisions of paragraphs 1 and 2 of this section, prizes may be offered for the highest scoring dogs of the Groups as defined in Chapter 2 of the Dog Show Rules, or for the highest scoring dogs of any breeds, but not for a breed variety. Show varieties are not recognized for obedience. In accordance with Chapter 2, all Poodles are in the Non-Sporting Group and all Manchester Terriers in the Terrier Group.

Prizes offered only to members of certain clubs or organizations will not be approved for publication in premium lists.

Section 33. **Risk.** The owner or agent entering a dog in an obedience trial does so at his own risk and agrees to abide by the rules of The American Kennel Club, and the Obedience Regulations.

Section 34. **Decisions.** At the trial the decisions of the judge shall be final in all matters affecting the scoring and the working of the dogs and their handlers. The Obedience Trial Committee, or the Bench Show Committee if the trial is held by a show-giving club, shall decide all other matters arising at the trial, including protests against dogs made under Chapter 20 of the Dog Show Rules, subject, however, to the rules and regulations of The American Kennel Club.

Section 35. **Dogs Must Compete.** Any dog entered and received at a licensed or member obedience trial must compete in all exercises of all classes in which it is entered unless disqualified, expelled, or excused by the judge or by the Bench Show or Obedience Trial Committee, or unless excused by the official veterinarian to protect the health of the dog or of other dogs at the trial. The excuse of the official veterinarian must be in writing and must be approved by the Superintendent or Show or Trial Secretary, and must be submitted to The American Kennel Club with the report of the trial. The judge must report to The American Kennel Club any dog that is not brought back for the group exercises.

Section 36. **Judging Program.** Any club holding a licensed or member obedience trial must prepare, after the entries have closed, a program showing the time scheduled for the judging of each of the classes. A copy of this program shall be mailed to the owner of each entered dog and to each judge, and the program shall be printed in the catalog. This program shall be based on the judging of no more than 8 Novice entries, 7 Open entries, or 5 Utility entries, per hour during the time the show or trial will be open as published in the premium list, taking into consideration the starting hour for judging if published in the premium list, and the availability of rings. In addition, one hour for rest or meals must be allowed if, under this formula, it will take more than five hours of actual judging to judge the dogs entered under him. No judge shall be assigned to judge for more than eight hours in one day under this formula, including any breed judging assignment if the obedience trial is held in conjunction with a dog show.

If any non-regular class is to be judged in the same ring as any regular class, or by the judge of any regular class, the non-regular class must be judged after the regular class.

Section 37. **Limitation of Entries.** If a club anticipates an entry in excess of its facilities for a licensed or member trial, it may limit entries in any or all regular classes, but non-regular classes will not be approved if the facilities are limited; or a club may limit entries in any or all regular classes to 64 in a Novice class, 56 in an Open class, or 40 in a Utility class.

Prominent announcement of such limits must appear on the title or cover page of the premium list for an obedience trial or immediately under the obedience heading in the premium list for a dog show, with a statement that entries in one or more specified classes or in the obedience trial will automatically close when a certain limit or limits have been reached, even though the official closing date for entries has not arrived.

Section 38. **Additional Judges, Reassignment, Split Classes.** If when the entries have closed, it is found that the entry under one or more judges exceeds the limit established in Section 36, the club shall immediately secure the approval of The American Kennel Club for the appointment of one or more additional judges, or for reassignment of its advertised judges, so that no judge will be required to exceed the limit.

If a judge with an excessive entry was advertised to judge more than one class, one or more of his classes shall be assigned to another judge. The class or classes selected for reassignment shall first be any non-regular classes for which he was advertised, and shall then be either the regular class or classes with the minimum number of entries, or those with the minimum scheduled time, which will bring the advertised judge's schedule within, and as close as possible to, the maximum limit. If a judge with an excessive entry was advertised to judge only one class, the Superintendent, Show Secretary, or Obedience Trial Secretary, shall divide the entry as evenly as possible between the advertised judge and the other judge by drawing lots.

The club shall promptly mail to the owner of each entry affected, a notification of any change of judge. The owner shall be permitted to withdraw such entry at any time prior to the day of the show, and the entry fee shall then be refunded. If the entry in any one class is split in this manner, the advertised judge shall judge the run-off of any tie scores that may develop between the two groups of dogs, after each judge has first run-off any ties resulting from his own judging.

Section 39. **Split Classes in Premium List.** A club may choose to announce two or more judges for any class in its premium list. In such case the entries shall be divided by lots as provided above. The identification slips and judging program shall be made up so that the owner of each dog will know the division, and the judge of the division, in which his dog is entered, but no owner shall be entitled to a refund of entry fee. In such case the premium list shall also specify the judge for the run-off of any tie scores which may develop between the dogs in the different groups, after each judge has first run-off any ties resulting from his own judging.

Section 40. Split Classes, Official Ribbons. A club which gives a split class, whether the split is announced in the premium list or made after entries have closed, shall not award American Kennel Club official ribbons in either section, but may offer prizes on the basis of qualifying scores made within each section if the split class is announced in the premium list. The four dogs with the highest qualifying scores in the class regardless of the section in which they were made, shall be called back into the ring and awarded the four American Kennel Club official ribbons by one of the judges of the class who shall be responsible for recording the entry numbers of the four placed dogs in one of the judges' books.

Section 41. Training of Dogs. There shall be no drilling nor intensive or corrective training of dogs on the grounds or premises at a licensed or member obedience trial. No practice rings or areas shall be permitted at such events. All dogs shall be kept on leash except when in the obedience ring or exercise ring. Spiked or other special training collars shall not be used on the grounds or premises at an obedience trial or match. These requirements shall not be interpreted as preventing a handler from moving normally about the grounds or premises with his dog at heel on leash, nor from giving such signals or such commands in a normal tone, as are necessary and usual in everyday life in heeling a dog or making it stay, but physical or verbal disciplining of dogs shall not be permitted except to a reasonable extent in the case of an attack on a person or another dog. The Superintendent, or Show or Trial Secretary, and the members of the Bench Show or Obedience Trial Committee, shall be responsible for compliance with this section, and shall investigate any reports of infractions.

Section 42. Abuse of Dogs. The Bench Show or Obedience Trial Committee shall also investigate any reports of abuse of dogs or severe disciplining of dogs on the grounds or premises of a show, trial, or match. Any person who, at a licensed or member obedience trial, conducts himself in such manner or in any other manner prejudicial to the best interests of the sport, or who fails to comply with the requirements of Section 41 above after receiving a warning, shall be dealt with promptly, during the trial if possible, after the offender has been notified of the specific charges against him, and has been given an opportunity to be heard in his own defense in accordance with Section 43 below.

Article XII Section 2 of the Constitution and By-Laws of The American Kennel Club provides:

Section 43. Discipline. The Bench Show, Obedience Trial or Field Trial Committee of a club or association shall have the right to suspend any person from the privileges of The American Kennel Club for conduct prejudicial to the best interests of pure-bred dogs, dog shows, obedience trials, field trials or The American Kennel Club, alleged to have occurred in connection with or during the progress of its show, obedience trial or field trial, after the alleged offender has been given an opportunity to be heard.

Notice in writing must be sent promptly by registered mail by the Bench Show, Obedience Trial or Field Trial Committee to the person suspended and a duplicate notice giving the name and address of the person suspended and full details as to the reasons for the suspension must be forwarded to The American Kennel Club within seven days.

An appeal may be taken from a decision of a Bench Show, Obedience Trial or Field Trial Committee. Notice in writing claiming such appeal together with a deposit of five ($5.00) dollars must be sent to The American Kennel Club within thirty days after the date of suspension. The Board of Directors may itself hear said appeal or may refer it to a committee of the Board, or to a Trial Board to be heard. The deposit shall become the property of The American Kennel Club if the decision is confirmed, or shall be returned to the appellant if the decision is not confirmed.

(See Guide for Bench Show and Obedience Trial Committees in Dealing with Misconduct at Dog Shows and Obedience Trials for proper procedure at licensed or member obedience trials.)

(The Committee at a Sanctioned event does not have this power of suspension, but must investigate any allegation of such conduct and forward a complete and detailed report of any such incident to The American Kennel Club.)

CHAPTER 2

Regulations for Performance

Section 1. **Ring Conditions.** If the judging takes place indoors the ring should be rectangular and should be about 35' wide and 50' long for all obedience classes. In no case shall the ring for a Utility class be less than 35' by 50', and in no case shall the ring for a Novice or Open class be less than 30' by 40'. The floor shall have a surface or covering that provides firm footing for the largest dogs, and rubber or similar non-slip material must be laid for the take off and landing at all jumps unless the surface, in the judge's opinion, is such as not to require it. At an outdoor show or trial the rings shall be about 40' wide and 50' long. The ground shall be clean and level, and the grass, if any, shall be cut short. The Club and Superintendent are responsible for providing, for the Open classes, an appropriate place approved by the judge, for the handlers to go completely out of sight of their dogs. If inclement weather at an outdoor trial necessitates the judging of obedience under shelter, the requirements as to ring size may be waived.

Section 2. **Obedience Rings at Dog Shows.** At an outdoor dog show a separate ring or rings shall be provided for obedience, and a sign forbidding anyone to permit any dog to use the ring, except when being judged, shall be set up in each such ring by the Superintendent or Show Secretary. It shall be his duty as well as that of the Show Committee to enforce this regulation. At an indoor show where limited space does not permit the exclusive use of any ring for obedience, the same regulation will apply after the obedience rings have been set up. At a dog show the material used for enclosing the obedience rings for the regular classes shall be at least equal to the material used for enclosing the breed rings. The ring must be thoroughly cleaned before the obedience judging starts if it has previously been used for breed judging.

Section 3. **Compliance with Regulations and Standards.** In accordance with the certification on the entry form, the handler of each dog and the person signing each entry form must be familiar with the Obedience Regulations applicable to the class in which the dog is entered. A handler with a physical handicap may compete, provided he can move himself about the ring as required, without physical assistance or guidance from another person, except for guidance to the proper location in the ring which may be given by the judge or, in the group exercises, by a person who is handling a competing dog in the ring.

Section 4. **Praise and Handling between Exercises.** Praise and patting are allowed between exercises, but points must be deducted from the total score for a dog that is not under reasonable control while being praised. A handler must not carry or offer food in the ring.
Imperfections in heeling between exercises will not be judged. In the Novice classes the dog may be guided gently by the collar between exercises and to get it into proper position for the next exercise. There shall be a substantial penalty for any dog that is picked up or carried at any time in the obedience ring, and for a dog in the Open or Utility classes that is not readily controllable or that is physically controlled at any time, except for permitted patting between exercises, and posing, or if the judge requests the handler to hold his dog for measuring. Minor penalties shall be imposed for a dog that does not respond promptly to its handler's commands or signals between exercises in the Open and Utility classes.

Section 5. **Use of Leash.** All dogs shall be kept on leash except when in the obedience ring or exercise ring. Dogs should be brought into the ring and taken out of the ring on leash. Dogs may be kept on leash in the ring when brought in to receive awards, and when waiting in the ring before and after the group exercises. The leash shall be left on the judge's table between the individual exercises, and during all exercises except the Heel on Leash and group exercises. The leash may be of fabric or leather and, in the Novice classes, shall be of sufficient length to provide adequate slack in the Heel on Leash exercise.

Section 6. **Collars.** Dogs in the obedience ring must wear well-fitting plain buckle or slip collars of leather, fabric, or chain. Fancy collars, spiked collars or other special training collars, or collars that are either too tight or so large that they hang down unreasonably in front of the dogs, are not permitted, nor may there be anything hanging from the collars.

Section 7. **Misbehavior.** Any disciplining by the handler in the ring, any display of fear or nervousness by the dog, or any uncontrolled behavior of the dog such as snapping, barking, relieving itself in the ring, or running away from its handler, whether it occurs during an exercise, between exercises, or before or after judging, must be penalized according to the seriousness of the misbehavior, and the judge may expel or excuse the dog from further competition in the class. If such behavior occurs during an exercise, the penalty must first be applied to the score for that exercise. Should the penalty be greater than the value of the exercise during which it is incurred, the additional points shall be deducted from the total score under Misbehavior. If such behavior occurs before or after the judging or between exercises, the entire penalty shall be deducted from the total score.

Section 8. **Commands and Signals.** Whenever a command or signal is mentioned in these regulations, a single command or signal only may be given by the handler, and any extra commands or signals must be penalized; except that whenever the regulations specify "command and/or signal" the handler may give either one or the other or both command and signal simultaneously. When a signal is permitted and given, it must be a single gesture with one arm and hand only, and the arm must immediately be returned to a natural position. Delay in following a judge's order to give a command or signal must be penalized, unless the delay is directed by the judge because of some distraction or interference.

The signal for downing a dog may be given either with the arm raised or with a down swing of the arm, but any pause in holding the arm upright followed by a down swing of the arm will be considered an additional signal.

Signaling correction to a dog is forbidden and must be penalized. Signals must be inaudible and the handler must not touch the dog. Any unusual noise or motion may be considered to be a signal. Movements of the body shall be considered additional signals except that a handler may bend as far as necessary to bring his hand on a level with the dog's eyes in giving a signal to a dog in the heel position, and that in the Directed Retrieve exercise the body and knees may be bent to the extent necessary to give the direction to the dog. Whistling or the use of a whistle is prohibited.

The dog's name may be used once immediately before any verbal command or before a verbal command and signal when these regulations permit command and/or signal. The name shall not be used with any signal not given simultaneously with a verbal command. The dog's name, when given immediately before a verbal command, shall not be considered as an additional command, but a dog that responds to its name without waiting for the verbal command shall be scored as having anticipated the command. The dog should never anticipate the handler's directions, but must wait for the appropriate commands and/or signals. Moving forward at heel without any command or signal other than the natural movement of the handler's left leg, shall not be considered as anticipation.

Loud commands by handlers to their dogs create a poor impression of obedience and should be avoided. Shouting is not necessary even in a noisy place if the dog is properly trained to respond to a normal tone of voice. Commands which in the judge's opinion are excessively loud will be penalized.

Section 9. **Heel Position.** The heel position as used in these regulations, whether the dog is sitting, standing, or moving at heel, means that the dog shall be straight in line with the direction in which the handler is facing, at the handler's left side, and as close as practicable to the handler's left leg without crowding, permitting the handler freedom of motion at all times. The area from the dog's head to shoulder shall be in line with the handler's left hip.

Section 10. **Heel on Leash.** The handler shall enter the ring with his dog on a loose leash and shall stand still with the dog sitting in the heel position until the judge asks if the handler is ready and then gives the order "Forward". The handler may give the command or signal to Heel, and shall start walking briskly and in a natural manner with the dog on loose leash. The dog shall walk close to the left side of the handler without crowding, permitting the handler freedom of motion at all times. At each order to "Halt", the handler will stop and his dog shall sit straight and smartly in the Heel position without command or signal and shall not move until the handler again moves forward on order from the judge. It is permissible after each Halt before moving again, for the handler to give the command or signal to Heel.

The leash may be held in either hand or in both hands, at the handler's option, provided the hands are in a natural position. However, the handler and dog will be penalized if, in the judge's opinion, the leash is used to signal or give assistance to the dog.

Any tightening or jerking of the leash or any act, signal or command which in the opinion of the judge gives the dog assistance shall be penalized. The judge will give the orders "Forward", "Halt", "Right turn", "Left turn", "About turn", "Slow", "Normal", and "Fast", which order signifies that both the handler and dog must run, changing pace and moving forward at noticeably accelerated speed. These orders may be given in any sequence and may be repeated if necessary. In executing the About Turn, the handler will do a Right About Turn in all cases. The judge will say "Exercise finished" after the heeling and then "Are you ready?" before starting the Figure Eight.

The judge will order the handler to execute the

"Figure Eight" which signifies that the handler may give the command or signal to Heel and, with his dog in the heel position, shall walk around and between the two stewards who shall stand about 8 feet apart, or if there is only one steward, shall walk around and between the judge and the steward. The Figure Eight in the Novice classes shall be done on leash only. The handler may choose to go in either direction. There shall be no About Turn in the Figure Eight, but the handler and dog shall go twice completely around the Figure Eight with at least one Halt during and another Halt at the end of the exercise.

Section 11. **Stand for Examination.** The judge will give the order for examination and the handler, without further order from the judge, will stand or pose his dog off leash, give the command and/or signal to Stay, walk forward about six feet in front of his dog, turn around, and stand facing his dog. The method by which the dog is made to stand or pose is optional with the handler who may take any reasonable time in posing the dog, as in the show ring, before deciding to give the command and/or signal to Stay. The judge will approach the dog from the front and will touch its head, body and hindquarters only, and will then give the order "Back to your dog", whereupon the handler will walk around behind his dog to the heel position. The dog must remain in a standing position until the judge says "Exercise finished". The dog must show no shyness nor resentment at any time during the exercise.

Section 12. **Heel Free.** This shall be executed in the same manner as Heel on Leash except that the dog is off the leash. Heeling in both Novice and Open classes is done in the same manner except that in the Open classes all work is done off leash, including the Figure Eight.

Section 13. **Recall and Drop on Recall.** To execute the Recall to handler, upon order or signal from the judge "Leave your dog", the dog is given the command and/or signal to stay in the sitting position while the handler walks forward about 35 feet towards the other end of the ring, turns around, and faces his dog. Upon order or signal from the judge "Call your dog", the handler calls or signals the dog, which in the Novice class must come straight in at a brisk pace and sit straight, centered immediately in front of the handler's feet and close enough so that the handler could readily touch its head without moving either foot or having to stretch forward. The dog shall not touch the handler nor sit between his feet. Upon order or signal from the judge to "Finish", the dog on command or signal must go smartly to the heel position and sit. The method by which the dog goes to the heel position shall be optional with the handler provided it is done smartly and the dog sits straight at heel.

In the Open class, at a point designated by the judge, the dog must drop completely to a down position immediately on command or signal from the handler, and must remain in the down position until, on order or signal from the judge, the handler calls or signals the dog which must rise and complete the exercise as in the Novice class.

Section 14. **Long Sit.** In the Long Sit in the Novice classes all the competing dogs in the class take the exercise together, except that if there are 12 or more dogs they shall, at the judge's option, be judged in groups of not less than 6 nor more than 15 dogs. Where the same judge does both classes the separate classes may be combined provided there are not more than 15 dogs competing in the two classes combined. The dogs that are in the ring shall be lined up in catalog order along one of the four sides of the ring. Handlers' armbands, weighted with leashes or other articles if necessary, shall be placed behind the dogs. On order from the judge the handlers shall sit their dogs, if they are not already sitting, and on further order from the judge to "Leave your dogs" the handlers shall give the command and/or signal to Stay and immediately leave their dogs, go to the opposite side of the ring, and line up facing their respective dogs. After one minute from the time he has ordered the handlers to leave their dogs, the judge will order the handlers "Back to your dogs" whereupon the handlers must return promptly to their dogs, each walking around and in back of his own dog to the heel position. The dogs must not move from the sitting position until after the judge says "Exercise finished".

Section 15. **Long Down.** The Long Down in the Novice classes is done in the same manner as the Long Sit except that instead of sitting the dogs the handlers, on order from the judge, will down their dogs without touching the dogs or their collars, and except further that the judge will order the handlers back after three minutes. The dogs must stay in the down position until after the judge says "Exercise finished".

Section 16. **Open Classes, Long Sit and Long Down.** These exercises in the Open classes are performed in the same manner as in the Novice classes except that after leaving their dogs the handlers must cross to the opposite side of the ring, and then leave the ring in single file as directed by the judge and go to a place designated by the judge, completely out of sight of their dogs, where they must remain until called by the judge after the expiration of the time limit of three minutes in the Long Sit and five minutes in the Long Down, from the time the judge gave the order to "Leave your dogs". On order from the judge the handlers shall return to the ring in single file in reverse order, lining up facing their dogs at the opposite side of the ring, and returning to their dogs on order from the judge.

Section 17. **Retrieve on the Flat.** In retrieving the dumbbell on the flat, the handler stands with his dog sitting in the heel position in a place designated by the judge, and the judge gives the orders "Throw it", whereupon the handler may give the command and/or signal to Stay, which may not be given with the hand that is holding the dumbbell, and throws the dumbbell; "Send your dog", whereupon the handler gives the command or signal to his dog to retrieve; "Take it", whereupon the handler may give a command or signal and takes the dumbbell from the dog; "Finish", whereupon the handler gives the command or signal to heel as in the Recall. The dog shall not move forward to retrieve nor deliver to hand on return until given the command or signal by the handler following order by the judge. The retrieve shall be executed at a fast trot or gallop, without unnecessary mouthing or playing with the dumbbell. The dog shall sit straight, centered immediately in front of its handler's feet and close enough so that the handler can readily take the dumbbell without moving either foot or having to stretch forward. The dog shall not touch the handler nor sit between his feet.

The dumbbell, which must be approved by the judge, shall be made of one or more solid pieces of one of the heavy hardwoods, which shall not be hollowed out. It may be unfinished, or coated with a clear finish, or painted white. It shall have no decorations or attachments but may bear an inconspicuous mark for identification. The size of the dumbbell shall be proportionate to the size of the dog. The judge shall require the dumbbell to be thrown again before the dog is sent if, in his opinion, it is thrown too short a distance, or too far to one side, or against the ringside.

Section 18. **Retrieve over High Jump.** In retrieving the dumbbell over the High Jump, the exercise is executed in the same manner as the Retrieve on the Flat, except that the dog must jump the High Jump both going and coming. The High Jump shall be jumped clear and the jump shall be as nearly as possible one and one-half times the height of the dog at the withers, as determined by the judge, with a minimum height of 8 inches and a maximum height of 36 inches. This applies to all breeds with the following exceptions:

The jump shall be once the height of the dog at the withers or 36 inches, whichever is less, for the following breeds—
　Bloodhounds
　Bullmastiffs
　Great Danes
　Great Pyrenees
　Mastiffs
　Newfoundlands
　St. Bernards

The jump shall be once the height of the dog at the withers or 8 inches, whichever is greater, for the following breeds—
　Spaniels (Clumber)
　Spaniels (Sussex)
　Basset Hounds
　Dachshunds
　Welsh Corgis (Cardigan)
　Welsh Corgis (Pembroke)
　Australian Terriers
　Cairn Terriers
　Dandie Dinmont Terriers
　Norwich Terriers
　Scottish Terriers
　Sealyham Terriers
　Skye Terriers
　West Highland White Terriers
　Maltese
　Pekingese
　Bulldogs
　French Bulldogs

The handler has the option of standing any reasonable distance from the High Jump, but must stay in the same spot throughout the exercise.

The side posts of the High Jump shall be 4 feet high and the jump shall be 5 feet wide and shall be so constructed as to provide adjustment for each 2 inches from 8 inches to 36 inches. It is suggested that the jump have a bottom board 8 inches wide including the space from the bottom of the board to the ground or floor, together with three other 8 inch boards, one 4 inch board, and one 2 inch board. A 6 inch board may also be provided. The jump shall be painted a flat white. The width in inches, and nothing else, shall be painted on each side of each board in black 2 inch figures, the figure on the bottom board representing the distance from the ground or floor to the top of the board.

Section 19. **Broad Jump.** In the Broad Jump the handler will stand with his dog sitting in the heel position in front of and anywhere within 10 feet of the jump. On order from the judge to "Leave your dog", the handler will give his dog the command and/or signal to stay, and go to a position facing the right side of the jump, with his toes about 2 feet from the jump, and anywhere between the first and last hurdles. On order from the judge the handler shall give the command or signal to jump and the dog shall clear the entire distance of the Broad Jump without touching and, without further command or signal, return to a sitting position immediately in front of the handler as in the Recall. The handler shall change his position by executing a right angle turn while the dog is in mid-air, but shall remain in the same spot. On order from the judge, the handler will give the command or signal to Heel and the dog shall finish as in the Recall.

The Broad Jump shall consist of four hurdles, built to telescope for convenience, made of boards about 8 inches wide, the largest measuring about 5 feet in length and 6 inches high at the highest point, all painted a flat white. When set up they shall be arranged in order of size and shall be evenly spaced so as to cover a distance equal to twice the height of the High Jump as set for the particular dog, with the low side of each hurdle and the lowest hurdle nearest the dog. The four hurdles shall be used for a jump of 52" to 72", three for a jump of 32" to 48", and two for a jump of 16" to 28". The highest hurdles shall be removed first.

Section 20. **Scent Discrimination.** In each of these two exercises the dog must select by scent alone and retrieve an article which has been handled by its handler. The articles shall be provided by the handler and these shall consist of two sets, each comprised of five identical articles not more than six inches in length, which may be items of everyday use. One set shall be made entirely of rigid metal, and one of leather of such design that nothing but leather is visible except for the minimum amount of thread or metal necessary to hold the article together. The articles in each set must be legibly numbered each with a different number, and must be approved by the judge.

The handler shall present all 10 articles to the judge and the judge shall designate one article from each of the two sets, and shall make a written note of the numbers of the two articles he selects. These two handler's articles shall be placed on a table or chair in the ring until picked up by the handler who shall hold in his hand only one article at a time. The handler's scent may be imparted to the article only from his hands which must remain in plain sight. The handler has the option as to which article he picks up first. Before the start of the Scent Discrimination exercises the judge or the steward will handle each of the remaining 8 articles as he places them at random in the ring about 6 inches apart. The handler will stand about 15 feet from the articles with the dog sitting in the heel position. The handler and dog will face away from the articles that are on the ground or floor from the time the judge takes the handler's article until he orders "Send your dog". On order from the judge, the handler immediately will place his article on the judge's book or work sheet and the judge, without touching the article with his hands, will place it among the other articles.

On order from the judge to "Send your dog", the handler and dog will execute a Right About Turn to face the articles and the handler will simultaneously give the command or signal to retrieve. The dog shall not again sit after turning, but shall go directly to the articles. The handler may give his scent to the dog by gently touching the dog's nose with the palm of one open hand, but this may only be done while the dog is sitting at heel and the arm and hand must be returned to a natural position before handler and dog turn to face the articles. The dog shall go at a brisk pace to the articles. It may take any reasonable time to select the right article, but only provided it works continuously and does not pick up any article other than the one with its handler's scent. After picking up the right article the dog shall return at a brisk pace and complete the exercise as in the Retrieve on the Flat.

The same procedure is followed in each of the two Scent Discrimination exercises. Should a dog retrieve a wrong article in the first exercise, it shall be placed on the table or chair, and the handler's article must also be taken up from the remaining articles. The second exercise shall then be completed with one less article in the ring.

Section 21. **Directed Retrieve.** In this exercise the handler will provide three regular full-size, predominantly white, work gloves, which must be open and must be approved by the judge. The handler will stand with his dog sitting in the heel position, midway between and in line with the two jumps. The judge or steward will then drop the three gloves across the end of the ring in view of the handler and dog, one glove in each corner and one in the center, about 3 feet from the end of the ring and, for the corner gloves, about 3 feet from the side of the ring, where all three gloves will be clearly visible to the dog and handler. There shall be no table or chair at this end of the ring.

The judge will give the order "Left" or "Right" or "Center". If the judge orders "Left" or "Right", the handler must give the command to Heel and shall pivot in place with his dog in the direction ordered, to face the designated glove. The handler shall not touch the dog to get it in position. The handler will then give his dog the direction to the designated glove with a single motion of his left hand and arm along the right side of the dog, and will give the command to retrieve either simultaneously with or immediately following the giving of the direction. The dog shall then go directly to the glove at a brisk pace and retrieve it without unnecessary mouthing or playing with it, completing the exercise as in Retrieve on the Flat.

The handler may bend his knees and body in giving the direction to the dog, after which the handler will stand erect with his arms in a natural position. The exercise shall consist of a single retrieve, but the judge shall designate different glove positions for successive dogs.

Section 22. **Signal Exercise.** In the Signal Exercise the heeling is done in the same manner as in the Heel Free exercise except that throughout the entire exercise the handler uses signals only and must not speak to his dog at any time. On order from the judge "Forward", the handler may signal his dog to walk at heel and then, on specific order from the judge in each case, the handler and the dog execute a "Left turn", "Right turn", "About turn", "Halt", "Slow", "Normal", "Fast." These orders may be given in any sequence and may be repeated if necessary. Then on order from the judge, and while the dog is walking at heel, the handler signals his dog to Stand in the heel position near the end of the ring, and on further order from the judge "Leave your dog", the handler signals his dog to Stay, goes to the far end of the ring, and turns to face his dog. Then on separate and specific signals from the judge in each case, the handler will give the signals to Drop, to Sit, to Come and to Finish as in the Recall. During the heeling part of this exercise the handler may not give any signal except where a command or signal is permitted in the Heeling exercises.

Section 23. **Directed Jumping.** In the Directed Jumping exercise the jumps shall be placed midway in the ring at right angles to the sides of the ring and 18 to 20 feet apart, the Bar Jump on one side, the High Jump on the other. The handler from a position on the center line of the ring and about 20 feet from the line of the jumps, stands with his dog sitting in the heel position. On order from the judge "Send your dog", he commands and/or signals his dog to go forward at a brisk pace toward the other end of the ring to an equal distance beyond the jumps and in the approximate center where the handler gives the command to Sit, whereupon the dog must stop and sit with its attention on the handler, but need not sit squarely. The judge will then designate which jump is to be taken first by the dog, whereupon the handler commands and/or signals his dog to return to him over the designated jump, the dog sitting in front of the handler and finishing as in the Recall. While the dog is in mid-air the handler may turn so as to be facing the dog as it returns. The judge will say "Exercise finished" after the dog has returned to the heel position. When the dog is again sitting in the heel position for the second part of the exercise, the judge will ask "Are you ready?" before giving the order "Send your dog" for the second jump. The same procedure is to be followed for the dog taking the opposite jump. It is optional with the judge which jump is taken first but both jumps must be taken to complete the exercise and the judge must not designate the jump until the dog is at the far end of the ring.

The height of the jumps shall be the same as required in the Open classes. The High Jump shall be the same as that used in the Open classes, and the Bar Jump shall consist of a bar between 2 and 2½ inches square with the four edges rounded sufficiently to remove any sharpness. The bar shall be painted a flat black and white in alternate sections of about 3 inches each. The bar shall be supported by two unconnected 4 foot upright posts about 5 feet apart. The bar shall be adjustable for each 2 inches of height from 8 inches to 36 inches, and the jump shall be so constructed and positioned that the bar can be knocked off without disturbing the uprights. The dog shall clear the jumps without touching them.

Section 24. **Group Examination.** All the competing dogs take this exercise together, except that if there are 12 or more dogs, they shall be judged in groups of not less than 6 nor more than 15 dogs, at the judge's option. The handlers and dogs that are in the ring shall line up in catalog order, side by side down the center of the ring with the dogs in the heel position. Each handler shall place his armband, weighted with leash or other article, if necessary, behind his dog. On order from the judge to "Stand your dogs", all the handlers will stand or pose their dogs, and on order from the judge "Leave your dogs", all the handlers will give the command and/or signal to Stay, walk forward to the side of the ring, then about turn and face their dogs. The judge will approach each dog in turn from the front and examine it, going over the dog with his hands as in dog show judging. When all dogs have been examined, and after the handlers have been away from their dogs for at least three minutes, the judge will promptly order the handlers "Back to your dogs", and the handlers will walk around behind their dogs to the heel position, after which the judge will say "Exercise finished". Each dog must remain standing at its position in the line from the time its handler leaves it until the end of the exercise, and must show no shyness nor resentment.

Section 25. **Tracking.** The tracking test must be performed with the dog on leash, the length of the track to be not less than 440 yards nor more than 500 yards, the scent to be not less than one half hour nor more than two hours old and that of a stranger who will leave an inconspicuous glove or wallet, dark in color, at the end of the track where it must be found by the dog and picked up by the dog or handler. The article must be approved in advance by the judges. The tracklayer will follow the track which has been staked out with flags a day or more earlier, collecting all the flags on the way with the exception of one flag at the start of the track and one flag about 30 yards from the start of the track to indicate the direction of the track; then deposit the article at the end of the track and leave the course, proceeding straight ahead at least 50 feet. The tracklayer must wear his own shoes which, if not having leather soles, must have uppers of fabric or leather. The dog shall wear a harness to which is attached a leash between 20 and 40 feet in length. The handler shall follow the dog at a distance of not less than 20 feet, and the dog shall not be guided by the handler. The dog may be restrained by the handler, but any leading or guiding of the dog constitutes grounds for calling the handler off and marking the dog "Failed". A dog may, at the handler's option, be given one, and only one, second chance to take the scent between the two flags, provided it has not passed the second flag.

The Club or Tracking Test Secretary, after a licensed or member tracking test, shall forward the two copies of the judges' marked charts, the entry forms with certifications attached, and a marked and certified copy of the catalog pages or sheets listing the dogs entered in the tracking test, to The American Kennel Club so as to reach its office within seven days after the close of the test.

CHAPTER 3

Regulations for Judging

Section 1. **Standardized Judging.** Standardized judging is of paramount importance. Judges are not permitted to inject their own variations into the exercises, but must see that each handler and dog executes the various exercises exactly as described in these regulations. A handler who is familiar with these regulations should be able to enter the ring under any judge without having to inquire how the particular judge wishes to have any exercise performed, and without being confronted with some unexpected requirement.

Section 2. **Handicapped Handlers.** Judges may modify the specific requirements of these regulations for handlers to the extent necessary to permit physically handicapped handlers to compete, provided such handlers can move about the ring without physical assistance or guidance from another person, except for guidance from the judge or from the handler of a competing dog in the ring for the group exercises. Dogs handled by such handlers shall be required to perform all parts of all exercises as described in these regulations, and shall be penalized for failure to perform any part of an exercise.

Section 3. **Judge's Report on Ring and Equipment.** The Superintendent and the officials of the club holding the obedience trial are responsible for providing rings and equipment which meet the requirements of these regulations. However, the judge must check the ring and equipment provided for his use before starting to judge, and must report to The American Kennel Club after the trial any undesirable ring conditions or deficiencies that have not been promptly corrected at his request.

Section 4. **Stewards.** The judge is in sole charge of his ring until his assignment is completed. Stewards are provided to assist him, but they may act only on the judge's instructions. Stewards shall not give information or instructions to owners and handlers except as specifically instructed by the judge, and then only in such a manner that it is clear that the instructions are those of the judge.

Section 5. **Training and Disciplining in the Ring.** The judge shall not permit any handler to train his dog nor to practice any exercise in the ring either before or after he is judged, and shall deduct points from the total score of any dog whose handler does this. A dog whose handler disciplines it in the ring must not receive a qualifying score. The penalty shall be deducted from the points available for the exercise during which the disciplining may occur, and additional points may be deducted from the total score if necessary. If the disciplining does not occur during an exercise the penalty shall be deducted from the total score. Any abuse of a dog in the ring must be immediately reported by the judge to the Bench Show or Obedience Trial Committee for action under Chapter 1, Section 43.

Section 6. **Catalog Order.** Dogs should be judged in catalog order to the extent that it is practicable to do so without holding up the judging in any ring for a dog that is entered in more than one class at the show or trial.

Judges are not required to wait for dogs for either the individual exercises or the group exercises. It is the responsibility of each contestant to be ready with his dog at ringside when required, without waiting to be called. The judge's first consideration should be the convenience of those exhibitors who are at ringside with their dogs when scheduled, and who ask no favors.

A judge may agree, on request in advance, to judge a dog earlier or later than the time scheduled by catalog order if the same dog is entered in another class which may conflict. However, a judge should not hesitate to mark absent and to refuse to judge any dog and handler that are not at ringside ready to be judged in catalog order if no such arrangement has been made in advance, nor if the dog is available while its handler is occupied with some other dog or dogs at the show or trial.

Section 7. **Judge's Book and Score Sheets.** The judge must enter the scores and sub-total score of each dog in the official judge's book immediately after each dog has been judged on the individual exercises and before judging the next dog. Scores for the group exercises and total scores must be entered in the official judge's book immediately after each group of dogs has been judged. No score may be changed except to correct an arithmetical error or if a score has been entered in the wrong column. All final scores must be entered in the judge's book before prizes are awarded. No person other than the judge may make any entry in the judge's book. Judges may use separate score sheets for their own purposes, but shall not give out nor allow exhibitors to see such sheets, nor give out any other written scores, nor permit anyone else to distribute score sheets or cards prepared by the judge. Carbon copies of the sheets in the official judge's book shall be made available through the Superintendent or Show or Trial Secretary for examination by owners and handlers immediately after the prizes have been awarded in each class. If score cards are distributed by a club after the prizes are awarded they must contain no more information than is shown in the judge's book and must be marked "unofficial score".

Section 8. **Announcement of Scores.** The judge shall not disclose any score or partial score to contestants or spectators until he has completed the judging of the entire class or, in case of a split class, until he has completed the judging of his division; nor shall he permit anyone else to do so. After all the scores are recorded for the class, or for the division in case of a split class, the judge shall call for all available dogs that have won qualifying scores to be brought into the ring. Before awarding the prizes, the judge shall inform the spectators as to the maximum number of points for a perfect score, and shall then announce the score of each prize winner, and announce to the handler the score of each dog that has won a qualifying score.

Section 9. **Explanations and Errors.** The judge is not required to explain his scoring, and should not enter into any discussion with any contestant who appears to be dissatisfied. Any interested person who thinks that there may have been an arithmetical error or an error in identifying a dog may report the facts to one of the stewards or to the Superintendent or Show or Trial Secretary so that the matter may be checked.

Section 10. **Rejudging.** If a dog has failed in a particular part of an exercise, it shall not ordinarily be rejudged nor given a second chance; but if in the judge's opinion the dog's performance was prejudiced by peculiar and unusual conditions, the judge may at his own discretion rejudge the dog on the entire exercise.

Section 11. **Ties.** In case of a tie for any prize in a class, the dogs shall be tested again by having them perform at the same time all or some part of one or more of the regular exercises in that class. In the Utility class the dogs shall perform at the same time all or some part of the Signal exercise. The original scores shall not be changed.

Section 12. **Judge's Directions.** The judge's orders and signals should be given to the handlers in a clear and understandable manner, but in such a way that the work of the dog is not disturbed. Before starting each exercise, the judge shall ask "Are you ready?" At the end of each exercise the judge shall say

"Exercise finished". Each contestant must be worked and judged separately except for the Long Sit, Long Down, and Group Examination exercises, and in running off a tie.

Section 13. **A and B Classes and Different Breeds.** The same methods and standards must be used for judging and scoring the A and B Classes, and in judging and scoring the work of dogs of different breeds.

Section 14. **No Added Requirements.** No judge shall require any dog or handler to do anything, nor penalize a dog or handler for failing to do anything, that is not required by these regulations.

Section 15. **Additional Commands or Signals, and Interference.** If a handler gives an additional command or signal not permitted by these regulations, either when no command or signal is permitted, or simultaneously with or following a permitted command or signal, or if he uses the dog's name with a permitted signal but without a permitted command, the dog shall be scored as though it had failed completely to perform that particular part of the exercise. A judge who is aware of any assistance, interference, or attempts to control a dog from outside the ring, must act promptly to stop any such double handling or interference, and should penalize the dog or give it less than a qualifying score if in his opinion it received such aid.

Section 16. **Standard of Perfection.** The judge must carry a mental picture of the theoretically perfect performance in each exercise and score each dog and handler against this visualized standard which shall combine the utmost in willingness, enjoyment and precision on the part of the dog, and naturalness, gentleness, and smoothness in handling. Lack of willingness or enjoyment on the part of the dog must be penalized, as must lack of precision in the dog's performance, and roughness in handling. There shall be no penalty of less than ½ point or multiple of ½ point.

Section 17. **Qualifying Performance.** A judge's certification in his judge's book of a qualifying score for any particular dog constitutes his certification to The American Kennel Club that the dog on this particular occasion has performed all of the required exercises at least in accordance with the minimum standards and that its performance on this occasion would justify the awarding of the obedience title associated with the particular class. A qualifying score must never be awarded to a dog whose performance has not met the minimum requirements, nor to a dog that shows fear or resentment, or that relieves itself at any time in an indoor ring, or that relieves itself while performing any exercise in an outdoor ring, nor to a dog whose handler disciplines or abuses it in the ring, or carries or offers food in the ring.

In deciding whether the faulty performance of a particular exercise by a particular dog warrants a qualifying score or a score that is something less than 50% of the available points, the judge shall consider whether the awarding of an obedience title would be justified if all dogs competing in the class performed the exercise in a similar manner; and must give a score of less than 50% of the available points if he decides that it would be contrary to the best interests of the sport if all dogs competing in the class performed in a similar manner on all occasions.

Section 18. **Orders and Minimum Penalties.** The orders for the exercises and the standards for judging are set forth in the following sections. The lists of faults are not intended to be complete but minimum penalties are specified for most of the more common and serious faults. There is no maximum limit on penalties. A dog which makes none of the errors listed may still fail to qualify or may be scored zero for other reasons.

Section 19. **Heel on Leash.** The orders for this exercise are "Forward", "Halt", "Right turn", "Left turn", "About turn", "Slow", "Normal", "Fast", "Figure eight". These orders may be given in any order and may be repeated, if necessary, but the judge shall attempt to standardize the heeling pattern for all dogs in any class. The principal feature of this exercise is the ability of the dog to work as a team with its handler. A dog that is unmanageable must be scored zero. Where a handler continually tugs on the leash or adapts his pace to that of the dog, the judge must score such a dog less than 50% of the available points. Substantial deductions shall be made for additional commands or signals to Heel and for failure of dog or handler to change pace noticeably for Slow and Fast. Minor deductions shall be made for such things as poor sits, occasionally guiding the dog with the leash, heeling wide, and other imperfections in heeling. In judging this exercise the judge shall follow the handler at a discreet distance so that he may observe any signals or commands given by the handler to the dog, but without interfering with either dog or handler.

Section 20. **Stand for Examination.** The orders for this exercise are "Stand your dog and leave when ready", "Back to your dog". The principal features of this exercise are to stand in position before and during examination and to show no shyness nor resentment. A dog that sits before or during the examination or growls or snaps must be marked zero. A dog that moves away from the place where it was left before or during the examination, or a dog that shows any shyness or resentment, must receive less than 50% of the available points. Depending on the circumstances in each case, minor or substantial deductions must be made for any dog that moves its feet at any time, or that sits, or moves away after the examination is completed. The examination shall consist of touching only the dog's head, body and hindquarters with the fingers and palm of one hand. The scoring of this exercise will not start until the handler has given the command and/or signal to Stay, except for such things as rough treatment of the dog by its handler or active resistance by the dog to its handler's attempts to make it stand, which shall be penalized substantially.

Section 21. **Heel Free.** The orders and scoring for this exercise shall be the same as for Heel on Leash except that the Figure Eight is omitted in the Heel Free exercise in the Novice classes.

Section 22. **Recall.** The orders for this exercise are "Leave your dog", "Call your dog", "Finish". The principal features of this exercise are the prompt response to the handler's command or signal to Come, and the Stay from the time the handler leaves the dog until he calls it. A dog that does not come on the first command or signal must be scored zero. A dog that does not stay without extra command or signal, or that moves from the place where it was left, from the time the handler leaves until it is called, or that does not come close enough so that the handler could readily touch its head without moving either foot or having to stretch forward, must receive less than 50% of the points. Substantial deductions shall be made for a slow response to the Come, depending on the specific circumstances in each case; for extra commands or signals to Stay if given before the handler leaves the dog; for a dog that stands or lies down; for extra commands or signals to Finish; and for failure to Sit or Finish. Minor deductions shall be made for poor or slow Sits or Finishes, and for a dog that touches the handler on coming in or sits between his feet.

Section 23. **Long Sit and Long Down.** The orders for these exercises are "Sit your dogs" or "Down your dogs", "Leave your dogs", "Back to your dogs". The principal features of these exercises are to stay, and to remain in the sitting or down position, whichever is required by the particular exercise. A dog that at any time during the exercise moves a substantial distance away from the place where it was left, or that goes over to any other dog, must be marked zero. A dog that stays on the spot where it was left but that fails to remain in the sitting or down position, whichever is required by the particular exercise, until the handler has returned to the heel position, and a dog that repeatedly barks or whines, must receive less than 50% of the available points. A substantial deduction shall be made for any dog that moves even a minor distance away from the place where it was left or that barks or whines only once or twice. Depending on the circumstances in each case, a substantial or minor deduction shall be made for touching the dog or its collar in getting it into the Down position. There shall be a minor deduction for sitting after the handler is in the heel position but before the judge has said "Exercise finished" in the Down exercises. The dogs shall not be required to sit at the end of the Down exercises.

If a dog gets up and starts to roam or follows its handler, or if a dog moves so as to interfere with another dog, the judge shall promptly instruct the handler or one of the stewards to take the dog out of the ring or to keep it away from the other dogs. The judge should not attempt to judge the dogs or handlers on the manner in which they are made to Sit. The scoring of the Long Sit exercise will not start until after the judge has given the order "Leave your dogs", except for such general things as rough treatment of a dog by its handler or active resistance by a dog to its handler's attempts to make it Sit.

During these exercises the judge shall stand in such a position that all of the dogs are in his line of vision, and where he can see all the handlers in the ring, or leaving and returning to the ring, without having to turn around.

Section 24. **Drop on Recall.** The orders for this exercise are the same as for the Recall, except that the dog is required to drop when coming in on command or signal from its handler when ordered by the judge, and except that an additional order or signal to "Call your dog" is given by the judge after the Drop. The dog's response to the handler's command or signal to Drop is a principal feature of this exercise, in addition to the prompt responses and the Stays as described under Recall above. A dog that does not stop and drop completely on a single command or signal must be scored zero. A dog that drops but does not remain down until called must receive less than 50% of the available points. Minor or substantial deductions shall be made for a slow drop, depending on whether the dog is just short of perfection in this respect, or very slow in dropping or somewhere between the two extremes. All other deductions as listed under Recall above shall also apply.

The judge may designate the point at which the

handler is to give the command or signal to drop by some marker placed in advance which will be clear to the handler but not obvious to the dog, or he may give the handler a signal for the Drop, but such signal must be given in such a way as not to attract the dog's attention.

If a point is designated, the dog is still to be judged on its prompt response to the handler's command or signal rather than on its proximity to the designated point.

Section 25. **Retrieve on the Flat.** The orders for this exercise are "Throw it", "Send your dog", "Take it", "Finish". The principal feature of this exercise is to retrieve promptly. Any dog that fails to go out on the first command or a dog that fails to retrieve, shall be marked zero. A dog that goes to retrieve before the command or signal is given, or that does not return with the dumbbell sufficiently close so that the handler can readily take it without moving either foot or stretching forward, must receive less than 50% of the points. Depending on the specific circumstances in each case, minor or substantial deductions shall be made for slowness in going out or returning or in picking up the dumbbell, mouthing or playing with the dumbbell, dropping the dumbbell, slowness in releasing the dumbbell to the handler, touching the handler on coming in, sitting between his feet, failure to sit in front or to Finish. Minor deductions shall be made for poor or slow Sits or Finishes.

Section 26. **Retrieve over High Jump.** The orders for this exercise are "Throw it", "Send your dog", "Take it", and "Finish". The principal features of this exercise are that the dog must go out over the jump, pick up the dumbbell and promptly return with it over the jump. The minimum penalties shall be the same as for the Retrieve on the Flat, and in addition a dog that fails both going and returning to go over the High Jump, must be marked zero. A dog that retrieves properly but goes over the High Jump in only one direction, must receive less than 50% of the available points. Substantial deductions must be made for a dog that climbs the jump or uses the top of the jump for aid in going over, in contrast to a dog that merely touches the jump. Minor deductions shall be made for touching the jump in going over.

The jumps may be preset by the stewards based on the handler's advice as to the dog's height. The judge must make certain that the jump is set at the required height for each dog. He shall verify in the ring with an ordinary folding rule or steel tape to the nearest one-half inch, the height at the withers of each dog that jumps less than 36 inches. He shall not base his decision as to the height of the jump on the handler's advice.

APPENDIX/207

Section 27. **Broad Jump.** The orders for this exercise are "Leave your dog", "Send your dog", and "Finish". Any dog that refuses the jump on the first command or signal or walks over any part of the jump must be marked zero. A dog that fails to stay until the handler gives the command or signal to jump, or that fails to clear the full distance with its forelegs, shall receive less than 50% of the available points. All other penalties as listed under Recall shall also apply. It is the judge's responsibility to see that the distance jumped is that required by these Regulations for the particular dog.

Section 28. **Scent Discrimination.** The orders for each of these two exercises are "Send your dog", "Take it", and "Finish". The principal features of these exercises are the selection of the handler's article from among the other articles by scent alone, and the prompt carrying of the right article to the handler after its selection. The minimum penalties shall be the same as for the Retrieve on the Flat and in addition a dog that fails to go out to the group of articles, or that retrieves a wrong article, or that fails to bring the right article to the handler, must be marked zero for the particular exercise. Substantial deductions shall be made for a dog that picks up a wrong article, even though it puts it down again immediately, and for any roughness by the handler in imparting his scent to the dog. Minor or substantial deductions, depending on the circumstances in each case, shall be made for a dog that is slow or inattentive, or that does not work continuously. There shall be no penalty for a dog that takes a reasonably long time examining the articles, provided it is working smartly and continuously.

The judge shall select one article from each of the two sets and shall make written notes of the numbers of the two articles selected. The handler has the option as to which article he picks up first, but must give up each article immediately when ordered by the judge. The judge must see to it that the handler imparts his scent to the article only with his hands and that, between the time the handler picks up each article and the time he gives it to the judge, the article is held continuously in the handler's hands which must remain in plain sight. The judge or his steward must handle each of the eight other articles as he places them in the ring. The judge must make sure that they are properly separated before the dog is sent so that there may be no confusion of scent between articles.

Section 29. **Directed Retrieve.** The orders for this exercise are "Right", or "Center", or "Left", "Take it" and "Finish". The principal features of this exercise are that the dog stay until directed to retrieve, that it go directly to the designated glove, and that it retrieve promptly. A dog that fails to go out on command or that fails to go directly in a straight line to the glove designated, or that fails to retrieve the glove, shall be marked zero. A dog that goes to retrieve before the command is given or that does not return promptly with the glove sufficiently close so that the handler can readily take it without moving either foot or stretching forward, must receive less than 50% of the available points. Depending on the specific circumstances in each case, minor or substantial deductions shall be made for touching the dog or for excessive movements in getting it to turn at heel facing the designated glove. All of the other penalties as listed under Retrieve on the Flat shall also apply.

Section 30. **Signal Exercise.** The orders for this exercise are "Forward", "Left turn", "Right turn", "About turn", "Halt", "Slow", "Normal", "Fast", "Stand", and "Leave your dog", and in addition the judge must give the handler signals to signal his dog to Drop, to Sit, to Come, to Finish. The orders for those parts of the exercise which are done with the dog at heel may be given in any order and may be repeated if necessary, except that the order to "Stand" shall be given when the dog and handler are walking at a normal pace. The signals given the handler after he has left his dog in the Stand position shall be given in the order specified above. The principal features of this exercise are the heeling of the dog and the Come on signal as described for the Heel and Recall exercises, and the prompt response to the signals to Drop, to Sit, and to Come. A dog that fails, on a single signal from the handler, to stand or remain standing where left, to drop, or to sit and stay, or to come, or that receives a command or audible signal from the handler to do any of these parts of the exercise, shall receive less than 50% of the available points. All of the deductions listed under the Heel and Recall exercises shall also apply to this exercise.

Section 31. **Directed Jumping.** The judge's first order is "Send your dog", then, after the dog has stopped at the far end of the ring, the judge shall designate which jump is to be taken by the dog, whereupon the handler commands and/or signals his dog to return to him over the designated jump, the dog sitting in front of the handler and finishing as in the Recall. After the dog returns to the handler the order "Finish" is given followed by "Exercise Finished". The same sequence is then followed for the other jump. The principal features of this exercise are that the dog goes away from the handler in the direction indicated, stops when commanded, jumps as directed, and returns as in the Recall.

A dog that, in either half of the exercise, anticipates the handler's command and/or signal to go out, that does not leave its handler, that does not go out between the jumps and a substantial distance beyond, that does not stop on command, that anticipates the handler's command and/or signal to jump, that does not jump as directed, or a dog that knocks the bar off the uprights or climbs over the High Jump or uses the top of the High Jump for aid in going over, must receive less than 50% of the available points. Substantial deductions shall be made for a dog that does not stop in the approximate center of the ring, that turns, stops, or sits, before the command to Sit, or that fails to sit. Substantial or minor deductions shall be made for slowness in going out, and all of the minimum penalties as listed under Recall shall also apply.

The judge must make certain that the jumps are set at the required height for each dog by following the same procedure described for the Retrieve over High Jump.

Section 32. **Group Examination.** The orders for this exercise are "Stand your dogs", "Leave your dogs", and "Back to your dogs". The principal features of this exercise are that the dog must stand and stay, and must show no shyness nor resentment. A dog that moves a substantial distance away from the place where it was left, or that goes over to any other dog, or that sits or lies down before the handler returns to the heel position, or that growls or snaps at any time, must be marked zero. A dog that remains standing but that moves a minor distance away from the place where it was left, or a dog that shows any shyness or resentment or that repeatedly barks or whines, must receive less than 50% of the available points. Depending on the specific circumstances in each case, minor or substantial deductions must be made for any dog that moves its feet at any time during the exercise, or sits or lies down after the handler has returned to the heel position. The judge should not attempt to judge the dogs or handlers on the manner in which the dogs are made to stand. The scoring will not start until after the judge has given the order "Leave your dogs", except for such general things as rough treatment of a dog by its handler, or active resistance by a dog to its handler's attempts to make it stand. The dogs are not required to sit at the end of this exercise. The examination shall be conducted as in dog show judging, the judge going over each dog carefully with his hands. The judge must make a written record of any deductions immediately after examining each dog, subject to further deduction of points for subsequent faults. The judge must instruct one or more stewards to watch the other dogs while he conducts the individual examinations, and to call any faults to his attention.

Section 33. **Tracking Tests.** For obvious reasons these tests cannot be held at a dog show, and a person, though he may be qualified to judge Obedience Trials, is not necessarily capable of judging a tracking test. He must be familiar with the various conditions that may exist when a dog is required to work a scent trail. Scent conditions, weather, lay of the land, ground cover, and wind, must be taken into consideration, and a thorough knowledge of this work is necessary.

One or both of the judges must personally lay out or walk over each track after it has been laid out, a day or so before the test, so as to be completely familiar with the location of the track, landmarks and ground conditions. At least two of the right angle turns shall be well out in the open where there are no fences or other boundaries to guide the dog. No part of any track shall follow along any fence or boundary within 15 yards of such boundary. The track shall include at least two right angle turns and should include more than two such turns so that the dog may be observed working in different wind directions. Acute angle turns should be avoided whenever possible. No conflicting tracks shall be laid. No track shall cross any body of water. No part of any track shall be laid within 75 yards of any other track. In the case of two tracks going in opposite directions, however, the first flags of these tracks may be as close as 50 yards from each other. The judges shall make sure that the track is no less than 440 yards and that the tracklayer is a stranger to the dog in each case. It is the judges' responsibility to instruct the tracklayer to insure that each track is properly laid and that each tracklayer carries a copy of the chart with him in laying the track. The judges must approve the article to be left at the end of each track, must make sure that it is thoroughly impregnated with the tracklayer's scent, and must see that the tracklayer's shoes meet the requirements of these regulations.

There is no time limit provided the dog is working, but a dog that is off the track and is clearly not working should not be given any minimum time, but should be marked Failed. The handler may not be given any assistance by the judges or anyone else. If a dog is not trailing it shall not be marked Passed even though it may have found the article. In case of unforseen circumstances, the judges may in rare cases, at their own discretion, give a handler and his dog a second chance on a new track. A track for each dog entered shall be plotted on the ground not less than one day before the test, the track being marked by flags which the tracklayer can follow readily on the day of the test. A chart of each track shall be made up in duplicate, showing the approximate length in yards of each leg, and major landmarks and boundaries, if any. Both of these charts shall be marked at the time the dog is tracking, one by each of the judges, so as to show the approximate course followed by the dog. The judges shall sign their charts and show on each whether the dog "Passed" or "Failed", the time the tracklayer started, the time the dog started and finished tracking, a brief description of ground, wind and weather conditions, the wind direction, and a note of any steep hills or valleys.

SUGGESTED CONSTRUCTION OF HIGH JUMP

FRONT VIEW OF HIGH JUMP

- 5'0"
- 1" x 3"
- 4'0"
- 2"
- 4"
- These boards are removable — 8", 8", 8", 8"
- Brace

SIDE VIEW OF HIGH JUMP

groove — top view of groove

1" x 3" brace

4'0"

This upright consists of two pieces 1" x 3" and one piece 1" x 2", nailed together, with the 1" x 2" forming the groove for the boards to slide in.

The high jump must be painted a flat white.

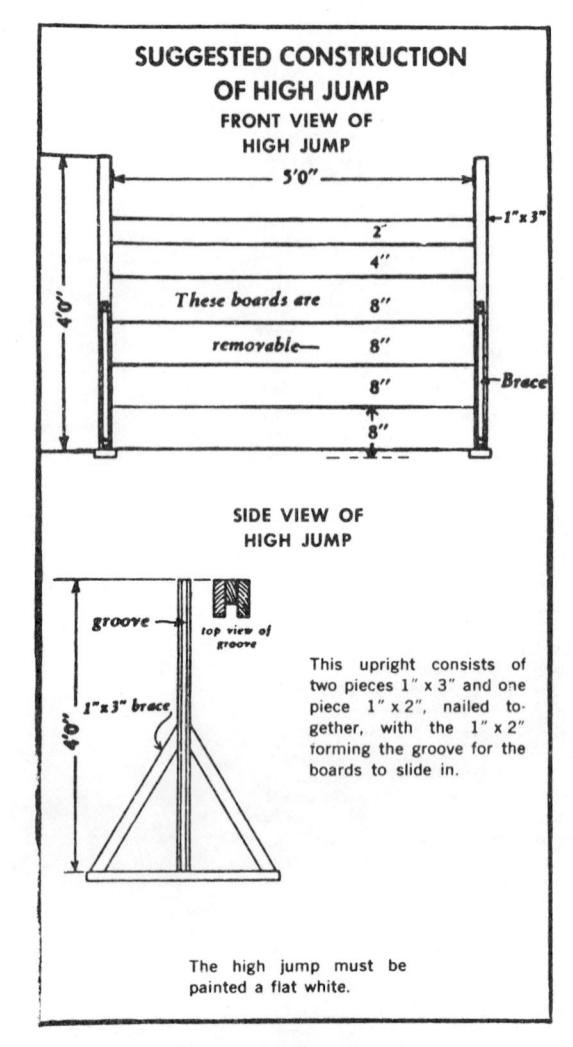

Minor changes are acceptable provided all requirements of Chapter 2, Section 18, are met.

APPENDIX/211

SUGGESTED CONSTRUCTION OF BROAD JUMP

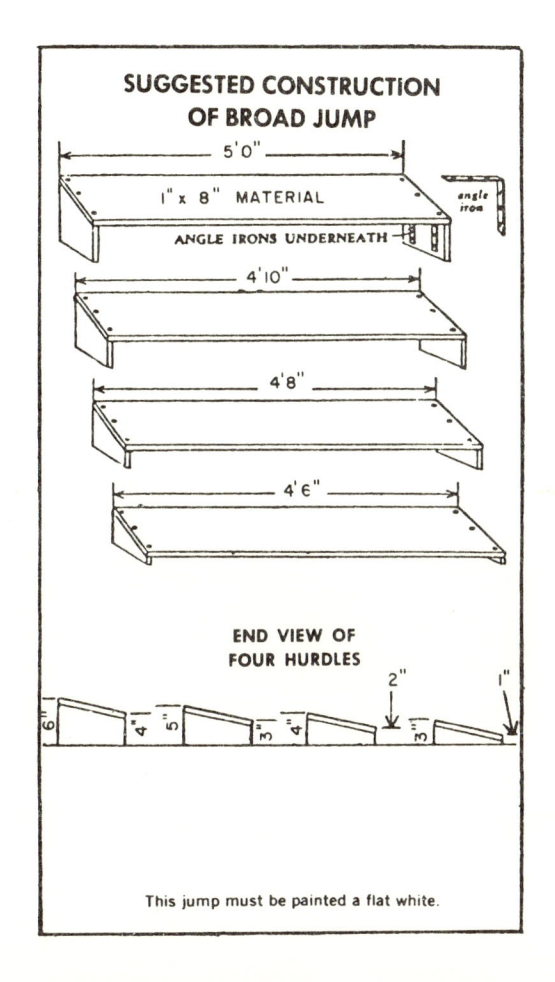

5' 0"
1" x 8" MATERIAL
angle iron
ANGLE IRONS UNDERNEATH

4' 10"

4' 8"

4' 6"

END VIEW OF FOUR HURDLES

This jump must be painted a flat white.

BAR JUMP. The construction of the bar jump should be similar to that of the High Jump illustrated. In place of boards, a horizontal bar is used which must be adjustable for raising or lowering according to the height of the dog.

Minor changes are acceptable provided all requirements of Chapter 2, Sections 19 and 23 are met.

Index

About turn, 33
American Kennel Club, obedience regulations, 189
Attack training, 183
Automobile, 174–76

Bar jump, 133–35
Bathing, 181
Broad jump, 136; length specifications, 137; on-lead, 137–39; off-lead, 140–42; problems, 142; construction, 211
Brushing, 22

Car sickness, 175
Chewing, 20
Children and dogs, 22
Coat care, 22, 178, 181
Collar, 20, 21, 27, 29
Come, 71–75
Crowding, 48

Directed jumping, 162; problems, 163–65
Directed retrieve, 166–68
Down, 61–63
Down stay, 63–64
Drop-hand signals, 83, 91
Drop on recall, 82–85

Dumbbell, 98; reaching for, 104; taking from ground, 105, 106; problems, 108; retrieving, 109–13

Exhuberant dog, 14, 15

Fast pace, 34, 41, 45
Feeding, 22, 181
Figure eight, 35, 39
Forging, 48

Guard dog, 184

Hand signals, 83, 91, 94
Heeling procedure, 31, 40, 42, 46
Heel position, 78, 79, 94
Housebreaking, 19

Indoor housing, 19, 178

Jumping. bar, 133–35
Jumping, broad 136–42
Jumping, solid 115–18; off-lead, 120–23; retrieve on-lead, 123–26; retrieve off-lead, 127–29; competition, 130; height specifications, 200; construction, 210

Kennel, 19

213

Lagging, 50
Lead, 24, 25, 27
Left turn, 34

Nail care, 178

Off-lead heeling, 42, 44
On-lead heeling, 40, 41
Outdoor housing, 18, 177, 178, 180

Pivot in front, 67, 78
Puppy discipline, 20
Purchasing, 17

Recall, 71–74; off-lead, 75–77; hand signals, 92
Retrieve, 109–13; directed, 166–68
Right turn, 33

Scent discrimination equipment, 145, 146
Scent discrimination procedure, 147–51; advanced, 152–55

Send-out, 156–59
Shy dog, 15, 185–87
Sit, 51–55; hand signal, 92
Sit-stay, 56–60, 86–88; out of sight, 89, 90
Slow pace, 34, 41, 45
Solid jump, 115–30
Stand, 65–70, 185

Taking dumbbell, 100–103
Teasing, 19
Temperament, 13
Timing, 13–15
Training schedule, 34

Vacation care, 181, 182

Walking with dumbbell, 104, 105
Watchdog, 183, 184
Wide heeling, 46

Yard breaking, 171–73